Profiles

Phyllis McCarthy, MBE, MSc.

Phyllis is now retired but has had a varied and active professional life, working in libraries, the tourism industry and education. She was a Senior Lecturer in Computing at a London University before retiring. She was awarded the MBE for services to tourism and employment in 1981. She has been active as a Spiritualist Medium since 1993, being a Christian Spiritualist herself. She has always had a strong interest in spiritual matters and in alternative therapies, having studied herbalism, reflexology and aromatherapy. With her sister, Stella, and friend, Lynn, she organises and runs workshops on meditation and crystal healing.

Stella McCarthy

Now retired, Stella's career included work in libraries, tourism and, finally, fulfilling a long held ambition to be a sub-postmistress, a post she gave up on losing her sight. Stella has always been psychic and has developed her gifts to help others, also serving Spiritualist Churches since 1993 as a medium. Stella trained as a healer with the NFSH, now the Healing Trust, and was active, not only as a healer but also in their teaching and qualifications programme. Stella organises and leads workshops on meditation and healing.

Lynn Buchan

Lynn is a Hospital Training Manager, and combines this with her voluntary healing work. She is a member of the Healing Trust and is a healer at a famous charitable Healing Sanctuary. She is also involved in organising and presenting Workshops on Healing. Lynn is married to Alastair and has two children and two grandchildren. Now approaching

I

retirement, she is looking forward to using all her skills in promoting this work which we all so believe in as well as spending more time with her grandchildren.

Acknowledgements

The authors wish to thank everyone who has helped and encouraged them with this book, especially Alastair Buchan for his technical support and his photograph on page IV, Rita Greer for her advice and illustrations, both the covers and the chapter headings and Matthew Buchan for proof reading the work. All the help was given freely and the art work donated, for which we are very grateful.

Published by Brother's Way, 2011.
All Rights Reserved

Email: booksatbway.gmail.com

www.brothersway.co.uk

Frontispiece Photograph by Alastair Buchan
Cover Design and Illustrations by Rita Greer

ISBN 978-0-9571346-0-7
Printed by: The Ask Group Ltd, ASK House, Northgate Avenue, Bury St Edmonds, Suffolk, IP32 6BB, England.

IV

Walk With Me

... the Path to God

Wisdom from Spirit

by

Phyllis McCarthy, Stella McCarthy & Lynn Buchan

Given through the mediumship of
Phyllis McCarthy

Book 1 in the Brother's Way series

Cover Design and Illustrations donated by Rita Greer

www.brothersway.co.uk

Walk With Me

Walk with me and I will lead you,
Together we will scale each height.
Come and we will part the mists,
Walk proudly to that golden light.
Walk with me and I will keep you,
Guide you, guard you, take your hand,
And, together we will get there,
We will reach that greater land.

Walk with me when the way is stony,
And the path seems dark and long,
For, hand in hand, we will traverse it,
I will take you, keep you strong.
We will pace the way together,
Fill this path with love and light,
We will journey ever onward,
Disperse the darkness, make all bright.

Walk with me for light will lead us,
Lead us forward, ever on,
Walk with me for love will speed us,
Love sustain us, urge us on.
Walk with me - see the pastures,
See the streams, see that land
Which is filled with God's own promise
Of a beauty of God's hand.

Walk with me and we will get there,
Together we'll take every step,
Savouring each little marker,
Savouring each little leap,
Knowing that all have their purpose,
All lead us to that place
Where, with love, Angels greet us,
And we will live in love and grace.

Walk with me, the path is open,
God's open arms are beckoning us,
And, together, we will reach them,
We will get there for we must,
For there are others coming after,
Who will walk where once we trod,
Walk with me to that great homeland,
Walk with me the path to God.

Table of Contents

Brother's Way

Brother's Way is a group set up to help every individual find their own unique pathway to inner development – their own pathway to God. It encompasses all creeds and none. We, at Brother's Way, believe that everyone is on a spiritual quest to discover their own true nature and to open, in their own way, to its beauty and fulfilment.

www.brothersway.co.uk

Foreword

This book gives extracts from recorded sessions of conversations with a spirit guide who identifies himself only as 'Brother' and has communicated through the mediumship of Phyllis McCarthy since 1989.

At first, the contact was made when Phyllis and her sister, Stella, also a medium, sat in meditation together, initially, every evening while the link was developing and they were learning to use it. Brother communicates through Phyllis, in a deep, but not unconscious, trance state. Phyllis describes it as if she were listening to the communication although she is aware it is her voice used. Brother's communications took the form of conversations with Stella. Phyllis states that she is able to ask questions in her mind and Brother speaks the answers.

In 2008, a small, weekly, meditation circle was formed in which Lynn and Alastair Buchan joined with Stella and Phyllis in their spiritual quest for knowledge and Brother communicated to the group after meditation sessions. The beauty and the wisdom of the words were such that the group felt they must be recorded, initially, for their own sakes and CDs were made of each subsequent session.

Each member of the group was struck by the fact that when listening to the words again, they seemed fresh and new. Lynn then started typing out the transcripts and it is from these that this book is formed.

Although the group are Christian, the wisdom and advice is relevant to everyone, regardless of culture or religion. It truly transcends barriers and is concerned with an individual's relationship with self, with all life and with God. In each of the following chapters, there is an introduction, written by Phyllis McCarthy, then a series of questions from circle members, Alastair and Lynn Buchan and Stella McCarthy, and answers, given by Brother.

The questions are shown in italics. The answers, shown in normal type, are transcribed from recorded sessions.

The poems and prose between chapters are also Brother's words.

This book is about a journey. You could make it YOUR journey. One thing is sure. It will be a unique one. Enjoy!

Chapter 1

Spirit Guides and Spirit Communication

"When a spirit guide comes into your consciousness it is never as a stranger. It is the culmination of discovery and joint experience bringing you to an understanding that enables a greater pathway of mutual service to open before you."

Introduction

Many people grapple with the idea of spirit guides so let's start with some frequently asked questions on the subject.

Spirit Guides

What is a Spirit Guide?

A Spirit Guide is a loving being who has chosen to walk with us and to help and support us on our pathway. No, he didn't get the short straw. He chose us, because as we learn through him he learns through us. We both form part of the same spirit family and have possibly worked together many times before in many different guises.

Do I have a Spirit Guide?

YES! Everybody does. We are never sent to walk this Earth pathway alone. We are, of course, responsible for every decision we make, but our guide will help us and be there for us but he can only support us, not drag us along. We always make the choices. We learn from each choice and we take the consequences of it.

What if I make a wrong choice?

Even what we see as a mistake is a learning experience that might lead us to a new understanding. We could well look back and say 'this was the turning point.' This is when I started to accept that I am not perfect so I make mistakes. But the 'mistakes' are massive opportunities because of the learning that comes from them. Your Spirit Guides will not interfere with your decision and neither will they judge or condemn. Always, they will uplift you, support you and urge you towards the way of light. They will rejoice with you at every new achievement.

Do I have more than one Spirit Guide?

Some people are aware of more than one at a time and others will tell you that their Spirit Guide changes at different times. Both may be true or they may all be different facets of the one loving spirit. After all, if you believe in reincarnation, you will accept that your Spirit Guide may have had many different physical identities spread over ages and countries. So, it is possible that what you perceive as a different guide may be the same one but expressing himself from the image of another physical life path.

Can I identify my Spirit Guide?

Sometimes, if you need to. Some people are quite happy to accept a symbol, or just a feeling, as a representation of their Spirit Guide. However, many find some form of detail easier to deal with and, if so, detail is provided. It's not always clear where this detail comes from but that is unimportant. If it helps us to develop an easy working relationship with our Spirit Guides then it serves a purpose. Remember, though, that it is a spirit link between our spirit self and the spirit who comes to us. It isn't a physical thing. Otherwise, how could a Tibetan converse with us in colloquial English? It is a spirit 'thought' link, brought into physical detail in a manner acceptable to our physical minds. Wonderful, isn't it?

In the following section, questions from circle members are shown in italics and all answers are Brother's words.

Identifying Guides

Stella: Sometimes spirit guides give us names and personal details and at other times, they do not. Why is this?

Earlier along the pathway there is a need to have a name and other personal details before accepting a guide. As you progress on the path, what was once a need is not a need any more, it is a desire that stems from the physical mind. If it would help in the pathway of service for a persona to be attached to a guide, it would be.

When you prepare to work with one whom you call a 'new' guide, there will be a gradual coming together while the connection is being made. As to the purpose, you have to go in trust and find out. You cannot have total knowledge before you have discovered and sufficiently experienced to reach the point of understanding.

Do not be downhearted when the knowledge seems elusive. Look how far you have progressed in knowledge upon this pathway in this lifetime. I tell you this lifetime is a grain of sand upon the desert of time. It is fleeting and swift but you can, even within your own perceptions, change so much and the change brings you into greater knowledge and understanding of your spirit identities and your spirit pathways.

Sometimes when you ask for physical detail to attach to a spirit guide, you are not asking from a need, you are asking from a want.

When a connection is being made, the need is to walk in trust and to wait until the time is right. When you have sufficiently experienced together the 'new' link will become clear. It will be the 'ah yes' moment 'why didn't I see that before?', but your need is to go in trust and wait in patience.

What has gone before has been the discovery and the experience. It is never a *starting* point but an *understanding* point which enables the working pathway to really open before you. The learning pathway that brought you to that point is always behind you. When a spirit guide comes into your consciousness it is never as a stranger. It is the culmination of discovery and joint experience bringing you to an understanding that enables a greater pathway of mutual service to open before you.

Working with Guides

Stella: How can we better work with our guides?

In time, all the learning and knowledge is turned into the outpouring of service, of love through service, of light which emanates from God through the service together.

It is never confined to the tiny physical existence that seems so great and real to you. That is always just a stage within it. The journey never starts within the physical life.

Physical existence is necessary for the pathway of service. You do not need the little details. All that is needed is the knowledge of the presence of each other and the link is made. Sometimes, the details of a personality that were necessary to you at an earlier stage can become a hindrance.

As you progress in your work together, you can release your guide to connect with you without that persona and to open to the other aspects that he is more than ready and willing to share with you in the great understanding that you have built together.

Learn to release in order to progress together. This is a mighty step on the pathway.

Stella: Brother, we learn from you. Do you actually learn anything from us?

Oh yes. There is nothing within God's realm that is not operating according to the universal law of giving and receiving. As I give to you to the best of my ability, you give to me the means to progress on my pathway. I believe every teacher in whatever form will say to you, ' I learn so much from those I teach.' It is you who have put the label 'teacher' on to me and, by doing so, you put the name 'pupils' onto yourselves.

We are all seekers and we are all teachers as well. And we all operate in many different forms. Now, all of you have undertaken a physical pathway for a purpose. You always assume that the purpose is one to lift you from what you think must be a lowly state to a higher one. But did not the Master Jesus walk the earth? Do you think He was at a lowly state?

Stella: Did the Master Jesus have a guide like we have a guide?

Oh yes. Did He not always say "truly man, truly showing us the way." As every man has a 'guide' so, too, must Jesus have had one. But the word 'guide' is just another label.

We are always learning from each other and using the experience of each other. Sometimes, a physical pathway is walked in order to empower the individual in the role that you call 'guide' to work with another group. Sometimes it is necessary to do that before the next phase of giving. We are constantly experiencing each aspect of any principle and that principle includes learning and seeking. There is so much more to life than you can see with physical eyes but you are still experiencing the belonging to spirit which brings so much more into your scope.

Clairvoyant Communication

Stella: When we are doing clairvoyance and bring back perhaps three generations, four at the outside, is that because that's as far as anybody living now has memory of? Some belief systems say that the form exists only as long as someone remembers you.

In clairvoyance you are seeking to demonstrate the continuity of life. The only way that can be done is if the image is in a recognisable form. It would be of no benefit to give an image from so far back into the depths of the family that it could not be proved or known. The whole purpose of the union in love is the reunion of beings who have known each other within the physical form. That, therefore, precludes these earlier generations you speak of.

The other part of your question was whether that is the same as the belief that you live only as long as someone remembers you.

I believe that has stemmed from an inability to fully understand the nature of physical life and spirit life. Indeed, it is in the attempts to divide them that many misunderstandings have arisen.

Your physical form, that bears a certain name and is a collection of matter, has a limited life. The matter is redistributed when it is no longer needed, at physical death. However, the eternal spirit continues to exist and will hold on to the image of the physical form while there are those still on Earth they connect with. But the physical is merely a vessel for the true self.

The belief you speak of has stemmed from the life of the vessel. The life of the vessel does not go on. The life of the true being within the vessel does. I believe the misunderstanding has come from a time when the true nature of life was thought to be the physical life and that life eternal related to the physical life. It is quite different from your mediumistic messages.

Stella: So when, in Judaism, they hold the special festival where they recite the names of their ancestors way back so that they may continue to live, in actual fact they are reciting the names of vessels that have passed away but their love will still go to the spirit that inhabited those vessels?

Yes, it is prayer that is given in love. Therefore the reason for it, the effects of it may not be exactly as they think, but the power, the goodness, the reality of that lives and will always live and, in a way, perhaps that is the truth of what they are doing.

There are many different belief systems. There have been many and I believe there will be many more. All of them are formulated from an understanding at one particular point. If they allow the understanding to change as it does continually, then they will go on. If they become as stone, unchanging within a belief that belongs to one point of understanding, at one time, then the belief system will become a prison. But all have the loving thought and the prayers within them.

Stella: Sometimes we are able to bring messages from those who have passed very soon after their passing but with others it seems there can be a long gap. Are there any rules governing that?

There are no artificial rules. Each pathway is unique and each way, in the strength of eternal love, can cross any boundaries of time and space.

When you say in clairvoyant messages that you describe people that are recognised, you are being shown an 'image' of their physical vessel because, without that 'image', how could they make themselves known? But it is 'image' that is impressed upon you.

Stella: When do we shed the image of the physical vessel?

The answer to that is when you are able to.

For some, that is very quickly and for others, it could be generations. It is whatever is necessary for any individual.

Stella: If a being is able to shed their physical personality quickly, does that mean they are unable to communicate with those within the physical world with whom they travelled and shared that physical journey?

It does not mean that at all.

Within spirit they communicate at whatever level is possible or necessary and the ones with whom they are communicating will see an image that they recognise even though that image may well have been given up by the actual being. In order to communicate with those still upon the earth plane they will project that 'image'.

Stella: My belief has always been that spirit speaks to spirit whether within the physical or not, even though you describe the vessel that last carried the spirit from the other side.

Yes, indeed, and everyone has their own means of interpreting in a form that they will recognise and understand and that is how your communication works.

Lynn: The people that Stella and Phyllis see, some of those could presumably have reincarnated.

Oh yes.

Lynn: But what they are seeing is the projection of the spirit that the loved one wants to see, even though part of that spirit may be on the earth travelling in another life.

Yes indeed. It is a wonderful system, isn't it?

Stella: I once spoke to a man about his father whom I thought had passed to spirit and he said he wasn't in spirit but he was very ill at that time. I was saying to him 'they ask that you go and make your peace' because they had not been friends.

The man was very close to passing and when that happens the spirit consciousness gradually takes over. During the transition, it is possible to communicate as if from spirit. During that time, the man you speak of was able to communicate with his son in a way that would not have been possible on a purely physical level.

As you come closer to understanding the true nature of spirit – which you are now – you will gain a greater understanding of the true laws of the Universe and the power of love. Rejoice in the growing understanding.

Working with Angels

Lynn: How do angels fit into our universe? How do people connect to angels and what is their role in life?

Angels are with each of us constantly. Angels are indeed pure beings of love. They have been called messengers of God because, in their pure love, they can help, almost be a filter because we cannot deal with the pure and boundless love of God and fit it into the little box which is the physical state. The angels bring that pure love into forms that can more nearly be appreciated. A necessary stepping stone, as it were, and their purpose is pure love. Their purpose is to bring us pure love, completely without judgement. Pure love.

How can you reach them? How can you know them?

This is another of those things that, in your spirit selves, you do know. You are not still seeking. They are part of your reality as much as the air you breathe within the physical world is part of your physical reality. You don't need to understand the air to breathe it and for it to help maintain your life. The same is true with the angels. You accept them as readily as you accept that air and yes, I do choose my comparisons well, for the air that you breathe is part of your physical life force and the angels and the angelic presence are part of your spirit life force.

The Silence of the Heart

In the silence of the heart, there is music,
In the silence of the heart, there is joy,
There is vision, there is brightness,
There is love and there is lightness,
In the silence of the heart.

In the silence of the heart, there is harmony,
There is rest, there is ease, there is peace.
In the silence of the heart, there is tranquillity,
There is beauty and joy and humility,
In the silence of the heart.

In the silence of the heart, there is oneness
With all creation that ever was -
Oneness with nature, oneness with spirit,
With all life and with God, within it,
In the silence of the heart.

In the silence of the heart, there is company,
There is a meeting place of souls,
There is love and there is unity,
There is joy in the community,
In the silence of the heart.

Answers to Questions

Know that all of the answers to all questions are there for us.

It is just that, sometimes, you have to find the questions
before you can find the answers.

Chapter 2

Meditation

"Those loving beings that walk, work, rejoice and suffer with you, they know and trust you. You must not reject that trust by saying 'I am not worthy'. God knows that you are. God trusts."

Introduction

Meditation is probably the easiest way available to us to find our own spirit links and learn more of our own spirit nature.

Some people call it finding the inner silence. Many questions are asked about the best way to meditate and we find that the answer varies for every individual. Some like to meditate alone, others prefer to join a group. Some like to meditate in silence, others like music playing. Some like to use a guided visualisation to lead them in to it and back from it. The answer is to experiment until you find the way that is right for you.

The next section gives Brother's answers to questions about meditation.

Learning through Meditation

Lynn: Sometimes in meditation we seem to reach an understanding of something and sometimes the parts seem very disparate. Can you help us with that?

Think of everything that you experience in your meditations as a little jigsaw. You have been given all of the pieces. When you manage to fit them together you will say, 'Well of course, why didn't I see that went there?', but before you actually make that breakthrough, they can look very disparate.

Every time, you receive some of the little pieces and, whether you are aware of it or not, ultimately the complete set - that is everything you need to bring you into a greater understanding, a wholeness.

How do you construct this wholeness, I hear you say? Well, that is for you to find out but everything you need is there.

16

If you can find the time and space to be objective, to let go of what you perceive to be self needs and are able to step away from them and go beyond them, you will touch your real needs. Because what you perceive as self needs at the moment are mainly from the conscious, physical mind and they are often very different from those which come from your spirit mind. Often those things that are perceived as needs by the conscious mind are motivated by fear because you are bombarded with fear as soon as you start experiencing within the physical body.

When you are able to step beyond the fear, the wholeness will be abundantly clear.

Freeing Yourself from the Need for Detail

Lynn: Why is it that sometimes we experience things in meditation that are so clear to us at the time but then we find we cannot recall or describe them?

Sometimes, when you are describing your little meditations to each other, you say there was more. You say I know I experienced but I cannot remember that part.

The knowledge of the experience is within you but you have released yourselves from the necessity to bring everything into a conscious form before you can accept it and that is a great step in understanding.

Often, you describe seeing birds flying or rising unburdened into a great light. These are attempts by your conscious mind to put images to the experience of freedom and release which fill you during the meditation. The true experience belongs to the spirit state. The physical detail is the mind's attempt to put images acceptable to the conscious mind to something that emanates outside of it.

What you are examining is one of the fundamental underlying premises and truths of God's universe, one of the fundamental building blocks. It is no less than that.

Be glad of the images but accept the experience and the inner knowledge of it and you will have mastered the power to release.

Creating Peace

Lynn: Why is it that sometimes after meditation we feel such a deep peace?

Sometimes in your meditations, you are able to open the door to your true, unconfined, spirit reality which allows you to replenish in the light, to regenerate and to bring your new understanding into your physical world and so change your perspective of it. You are able to remember doing it.

The reward for remembrance is peace, peace within you, peace around you. You open that inner pathway and allow the peace to envelop you and to radiate from you.

If you hold thoughts that are not peaceful, thoughts of turmoil or conflict, you close that door. Do not allow the doorways to close for there is such need to create the havens of peace in your world. When you create them, you allow the beings who can only operate within peace to walk in your world and to spread the peace. Indeed, you hold the key and that brings greater responsibility for its use. Always remember that, for there are many who walk with you and depend upon your creation of peace and love to do their allotted work.

Experiencing in Spirit Consciousness

Stella: You speak of experiencing from our spirit consciousness and of our spirit existing outside of physical time. How can this be?

While you are within your physical consciousness you tend to think that things happen in a linear sequence, one thing at a time.

While you are experiencing in trust and freedom in your meditational state you experience the reality of your multi-faceted existence and all of these facets are concurrent.

You are as real within your spirit state as you are at this moment within your physical beings. In fact your spirit state is the lasting reality. In time you will see what seem to be the solid barriers of your physical world as the illusions that they are.

You are able to experience sharing with the whole of God's realm. All you need to do is to take the step in trust, in love, in sincerity and in the knowledge that as others trust you, so you must trust yourselves. Your conscious mind says to you, 'you are not worthy'. It says to you, 'how is it that you can do that, of course you can't!'

Those loving beings that walk, work, rejoice and suffer with you, they know and trust you. You must not reject that trust by saying 'I am not worthy'. God knows that you are. God trusts.

You must learn to take yet another step in trust because you are starting to experience the beauty of God's realm. It is available to you now, but always for a purpose.

Within those times of communion with loving spirits you are recharged. You are renewed and then you have to walk down from the height, also in trust and trust that it is right to subjugate that consciousness and experience within your physical minds again for the purpose of your pathway within this existence.

Sometimes after a meditation you say, 'I had a wonderful experience but I don't know what it was!' What that means is that you have registered the emotions and knowledge of a true happening but have no images of it now to bring into your conscious mind. That is only because your conscious minds have no means to attach physical images to the experience. The experience is real. The problem is in allowing the detail of it into what you, at present, see as the order of your mind. That order is fine but it is one small part of your reality.

What you need to do now is to say to that part, 'I am glad of you, I recognise you, I am glad to use you but I am no longer going to allow you to block out the other parts which are now available to me'. Gradually your awareness will expand and you will see that you are part of a greater existence and then to realise that all is one. All you need to do is to see one step ahead for you cannot see the destination. That is part of the trust and the experience.

Experiencing Freedom in Spirit

Stella: Can we really ever experience the true freedom of spirit while we are still in a physical form?

Even though you are in physical form you are true beings of spirit now. Sometimes in meditation you are able to experience rising in light, soaring within spirit and experiencing universal love.

If you go in trust and let go of your physical restrictions you will reach new heights and experience in a different way. You may see different light, different forms and experience different movements. You will be acknowledging the reality of your beings in spirit and with that acknowledgement comes not only the acceptance of the experience itself but the ability to take it and express it within your physical lives.

You may experience life before physical form, life after physical form, life during physical form but all from within the freedom of the spirit. You may experience far more than you can yet appreciate.

You will meet with those of your spirit family who walk the pathway to light with you even though you are still in physical form. You will have found the key to the kingdom within you and having found it, you will never lose it. It is the means to soar above, to see life as it is, not just the illusion of life which is created in order for everyone to have the experiences and the opportunities that they need within a physical form. That is the true illusion. The reality is freedom, the love, the different light, the lack of fear.

What you will really have experienced is the life within you that is life everlasting, life within God. And that is true freedom.

Entering your rightful place in spirit

Lynn: Can we experience what you call our rightful place in spirit now?

In meditation you can all move into your spirit consciousness, your true spirit self. You can allow yourselves to be free from the constraints of the physical environment, without questioning leaps in time because time is the illusion. You can allow yourselves to go with open spiritual hearts and minds and to experience your rightful place.

You can open the doorway to many other places of learning, of experience, of understanding and of sharing. Places which enable you to differentiate even more your physical reality, which is transient, and your reality in spirit, which is eternal and limitless.

When you enter a physical body and undertake a physical existence, you are taking on limit. You do it for a purpose and the greatest purpose is to experience limit itself. Because only when you experience limit can you fully discover and understand limitlessness.

Look and You Will See God

Look - and you will see God,
Listen - and you will hear God,
Reach - and you will touch God - vibrant and living,
Stand - and you will feel God within - His peace, His power.
The power of God, in which all things are possible,
The real God - not a facsimile.
In sharing, there is God - God the creator.
God the source of love and light.
Not just words, but God in truth.

There is joy in sounds.
There is praise in sounds.
The sounds of nature - the music of God.
The humblest cricket and the tiniest blade of grass
As it reverberates in the breeze make a symphony
of praise, in which there is God.

Mankind sometimes says "Where can I find God?"
God is with you everywhere - not hidden.
He is there for all to see, to feel, to touch,
to experience and to use, for He is part of you.

Let every sound be the music of God.
Every sound you make can be a symphony of praise.
Just as the humble cricket, the tiny blade of grass, sighing in the
wind.
Sounds of joy, sounds of caring and compassion.
Every sound expressed with love.

Hear the music all around you, the music of
the other parts of creation - the rain caressing
the leaves of the trees, the gentle ripple of the waters.
Other symphonies - The music of creation.

Listen - and you will hear God,
Look - and you will see God,
Reach - and you will touch God,
Stand - and you will know God - His peace - His love.

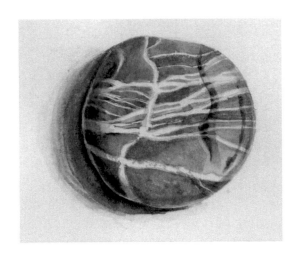

Chapter 3

Healing

"It may be that we have selected to go through the experience of a particular illness in order to help others, from within this life or from a spirit state. Many people have been set on a pathway of spiritual awakening by following a caring pathway. If there was nobody to care for, where would their opportunities for growth come from?"

Introduction

I have been interested in Spiritual Healing for many years and I am totally convinced of its power. However, I also believe that we are never completely passive instruments in any healing process. Even when Jesus healed we are told that he said, "Go and sin no more." And there can surely be no better role model for Spiritual Healers!

To my mind, by 'sin' he meant the imbalance that was at the root of the disease. For example, if you smoke and suffer from lung disease, then unless you give up smoking the healing must be limited. If you are eaten up by anger or jealousy to the extent that you suffer the effects of it, you cannot expect the Spiritual Healing to isolate you from those effects unless you deal with the cause. Cause and effect is, after all, one of the basic laws of the universe and a great spiritual enlightenment comes when we realise that.

Don't misunderstand me. I am not saying that if Spiritual Healing does not take away your illness, it necessarily means that you are not doing your part. I believe that before we take on a physical life we select challenges that are necessary for our spiritual development. Of course, we don't know from within this life what challenges we have chosen. It may be that we wish to experience overcoming an illness. I think it likely that anyone who is a spiritual healer will have selected this pathway at some time.

It may be that we have selected to go through the experience of a particular illness in order to help others, from within this life or from a spirit state. Many people have been set on a pathway of spiritual awakening by following a caring pathway. If there was nobody to care for, where would their opportunities for growth come from?

However, let us return to the question of self responsibility in healing. It seems that there is an inner need for the patient to open to the healing and allow the healing process to work. If so, how can it work with Absent Healing when the recipient has no knowledge of it, or in the case of babies and animals?

There is an answer to this apparent anomaly. I don't think that 'conscious mind' knowledge is necessary if, at the spirit centre of our being, we are open to the Spiritual Healing. I firmly believe we are spirit now. We don't have to wait for physical death to attain that state, but much of our true nature is closed to our conscious mind during a life path in order to focus on our essential experiences and challenges. We will never make sense of it from a physical perspective alone.

In the case of babies and animals, I believe they are always truly open to loving spirit. Babies haven't yet learned the lack of trust which 'closes' or restricts the links. I don't believe that animals ever learn to do that. So they are always open to receive Spiritual Healing and to allow its outworking in their lives.

Sometimes, Spiritual Healing gives us the peace and strength to cope with our challenges in this life and that is a very great healing. Brother often speaks of this and of the work of healers and the power of healing and answers our questions. This chapter is a selection of those questions and answers.

Focusing Healing on a Specific Group

Alastair: Is it possible to focus our healing onto one particular group, like, for example, children suffering from cancer?

Yes, it is possible to become a good channel for any specific group if the desire is there. Just as you feel drawn to that work, so, too, there will be those healing guides within spirit who are also drawn to that work.

It may well be that the purpose of being confined within a physical body is to be that outlet for healing for the group who have, perhaps, worked together within spirit to overcome a particular problem. It is necessary to have a physical outlet therefore one of the group makes the great sacrifice to enter into the confinement of physical life in order to be that outlet.

You speak of the many children suffering greatly before leaving the body and returning to spirit. You speak of some sufferings being so great that they do not wish to stay within the body. Let me speak of them just for a moment.

Many lives have been altered by the sacrifice of these bright beings. Sometimes the purpose is to add to the physical experience in order to lead to a breakthrough and therefore improve the lives of many coming after. For some, it is their suffering that has been a catalyst to changing the way of living, of thinking, the whole outlook and attitude of the many whose lives they touch.

There have been many people changing their ways because of often the short lives of these dear and advanced spirits who, like the Master Jesus, are prepared to suffer and sacrifice life in one form in order to enrich the life experience of many. And, yes, sometimes it is necessary for those around them to experience and overcome the pain and the loss. They need someone to give them that opportunity because without that experience they cannot advance upon their own pathways. There are many people whose lives have been so changed by the experience that they go on to help so many others despite their own pain.

Pain is a part of learning. It is a part of the physical way but what shines through it is the triumph of the human spirit, of spirit itself, over that pain. It is the triumph of the overcoming and the great strides forward taken in understanding because of it.

We do not learn anywhere near as much when we are on those points of life, those little plateaux, where we can rest and everything is bright and sunny. We learn through overcoming obstacles and scaling the heights and that does not come without pain.

Creating Healing Vibrations

Lynn: When we are healing, do we just create the vibration that allows spirit beings to come in to do what they need to do? Do we not need to do anything at all other than to make that link of love and create that vibration for it to happen?

Once you create the link of love and the healing vibration, all of the other things that people do are simply devices to help them. There is nothing wrong with them if that is what they find helps them to go into that calmness of being which allows the healing spirit to take over and do the work. Whatever anybody wants to do is fine but with the understanding of that comes the freedom to choose to do nothing.

Sometimes the person who comes for healing will feel more comfortable with something tangible happening. If so, then do something.

You see the physical activity is merely like a coat that is taken on. You put it correctly when you said that 'you create the means for spirit to do its work'. You work with that spirit, you are part of that spirit, not just a passive being enabling the work.

It is said so many times that the healer is a passive channel. It is right that you are the channel but much more than that, you are part of loving spirit, which includes the healing itself.

When the Master Jesus accomplished healing sometimes he simply said "you are healed". And sometimes there was action, but the action He knew was as a focus for the one who is receiving healing.

The answer is 'yes' and rejoice in the step in understanding. Each step in understanding opens your spirit channels that much wider and allows even greater connection, experience and then, even further steps in healing.

Loss of an Unborn Child

Lynn: In my healing work, I see many women who have suffered the loss of an unborn child.   What growth is in the experience for the spirit of the unborn child and also is this something that would be meant to happen or is this a mistake? Would it be something that was planned or is it just one of those things?

When a spirit life comes into the physical sphere there is always a purpose. It is never by accident. When it comes to entering a physical body and leaving it, the time is always known. However, this does not diminish the role of free will, choice and responsibility. Within that framework free will is paramount and choice is real in that at various points within any development there are two ways. When a choice has to be made, it is done so without the knowledge of how either way will unfold. No spirit is ever coerced into taking on a particular physical life path.   That, too, has always been freely chosen.

You ask about the purpose.   There are purposes for every being involved, however remotely. There is purpose for you, as you asked the question and now there is a purpose for each one who sees or hears these words, for they know of it as well. There is a purpose for the ones intimately involved, for the mother and there is certainly a purpose for the spirit who has, for what seems to you such a brief time, taken on the physical form.

I am able to give you some examples because they can be accepted by your physical minds now. There are others that

I could not express to you because you would not understand where the purpose is, or where it comes from.

It may be that the spirit being had a need, for some purpose of service, to re-experience the confines of the physical form even for a moment. Normally that is what you would call an advanced spirit being. Perhaps, for the next stage of their mission, it was necessary to experience those confines once more and, perhaps, for one so refined in vibration, a small extent of physical life is all that could be borne because the spirit is so pure it could not sustain for more than a very short time those heavier vibrations.

If it is that, then in spirit before coming to the Earth, the mother would have agreed to be the carrier. She would have agreed to go through that experience for the purpose of growth and understanding in order to help others. Only a very beautiful soul would be asked to be the carrier and would agree to be the carrier. It is, perhaps, impossible to see that fully from the physical standpoint.

Could I perhaps just liken that decision to the one taken by Mary, mother of Jesus, who before coming to the earth was asked if she could walk that pathway of pain, real pain, because it was necessary to find a way to bring the Master Jesus into the earth and on his mission. I know that He lived a longer time but it is a similar thing.

There can be many other reasons. It could be a need for the mother and child to touch in a physical manner because their spirit mission is together. It could be simply being served by loving spirit enabling a being to go through barriers of pain and emerge with a greater understanding. There are so many possible reasons, but none of them would make sense from the physical view alone.

Lynn: I think the thing that you are saying there is that actually it is planned, it is ordered. It isn't just one of things that happen. It was part of God's divine plan.

Yes and a part of a mutual service between the being who needed to experience physical existence for a short time and the lovely beings within the physical plane now. Mutual service that each of them understood before the physical journeys were undertaken but, of necessity, that knowledge is shielded from the physical mind or else the giving, the experience, is diminished.

It will be seen in its true and loving context when the time is right, but from spirit eyes. Remember there is a lesson in it for everyone, so each one of you is a recipient of the service of that great sacrifice.

Overcoming debilitating illness

Lynn asked Brother a question about someone who has suffered with a debilitating illness for some years. Before the illness he had a high powered and very stressful job. This answer is included because it could well relate to others.

Lynn: I know we cannot wave a magic wand.

But you know the magic wand is there and it is so very close. I understand that these words will cause frustration because they appear not to be helpful.

You see, we cannot take away the challenge but, because he has asked for direction, I will say to really think about fear. The conscious mind is fashioned by fear and the journey is to overcome that.

Sometimes someone has held to a belief that they fit into a particular 'box'. Perhaps the box is labelled, 'logical'.

I am not criticising logic but I am just trying to demonstrate the problem. Ideas have grown and a perception that this is what 'I' should be like. Perhaps a belief has grown that 'I must be first', not through any conceit, simply that that is my role, because I have put myself in a little box labelled 'logical and winner'.

Now perhaps those boxes have become prisons and, in their intensity, they are masking the other great achievements and potential and the other open pathways. For their rightful time they bought success, happiness and fulfilment and then a time came when, all of a sudden, these things became illusive. Instead of realising that those particular boxes might have served their purpose, the conscious mind – led by fear – says 'No this cannot be, there is no logic to it. Why, when everything I did pushed me ahead of the rest, why is it that not happening now?'

The conscious mind then said 'You had better go back into those boxes and find out what it is you have missed'. Sometimes when you can immerse yourself - or immerse the conscious mind - in the nice little puzzles in which it is happy, then everything is fine. But all that is happening is that you are going around in the same little circle while another part of you is screaming out and saying 'I have done this, it is passed, I want to go on'. But conscious mind so developed by fear says, 'No you can't go on, you have got to come back and find out where you went wrong'.

I would say to your friend, 'You did not go wrong. You took all the right steps, in discovery and experience and understanding. You achieved. You did all of that and you earned the right to come out of that state, because although it was once so comfortable it has now become a prison. You can walk out through it and say:

"I no longer want that type of achievement. I am no longer content with just the intellectual domain. I wish to take all of my main achievements, of which I am rightfully, joyfully proud, and take off these chains, walk forward unfettered as the true, sensitive being I am.

"I wish to experience not always winning on one level. I wish to experience not always dominating. I wish to experience the joyful opening of my spirit consciousness, putting aside fear and allowing this wonderful energy within me to flow through, to encompass me in its loving and peaceful light and to know that there is no pressure of fulfilment. I create that pressure through fear.

"I acknowledge that I fulfil the desires and needs of my true being, my spirit self, by putting aside that physical fear, and not being afraid to say I do not want that any more. I am content to start the process of learning again, starting from a point almost of anonymity."

If he could learn to put aside these unreasonable demands he makes upon himself, it would allow spirit energies to start to remove, replace and heal, so allowing the true beautiful spirit to emerge.

Using Crystals in Healing
'Discharge' Stone and 'Energising' Stone

Stella: We often use a crystal with healing because we think it enhances the power. Can crystals really help?

Indeed, the point on the crystal can capture the power of heaven and direct it within you. Or it can take the negative power from within you and discharge it into the earth where it can be dealt with.

Everyone has a 'discharge' stone and an 'energising' stone which is special to them. If you find your discharge stone, keep it with you always and then when you feel yourself becoming tense, stressed or fearful, take your discharge stone, touch it to your brow and to your heart and touch it to the ground. Then feel the negativity draining from you.

Carry with you, too, your energising stone. That will be charged with the power from heaven so touch it to any one of your energy centres. It will be a runaway for the negative and it will be an empowerment for the positive.

Select them well for they can be powerful tools.

Healing Prayer

Oh Great Spirit of Light, Our Father God, God within us.

Help us Dear Father to know and feel the true rhythm of life.
Help us to find the means to allow that rhythm to flow into
each world.

We thank you for our part in this wonderful chain of
creation. We ask that we may always make those choices
that will create good and healing. We thank you for the
many beings who help us on our way.

We ask that we in our own ways may help others too for
such is the rhythm of life, such is the rhythm of love and
such is the power of healing.

Dear Father we ask your blessing and your protection upon
and around all workers in light.

We ask that you keep them safe upon their pathways and
within the knowledge and awareness of the love within their
hearts and within their hands.

We ask in the name of the Master, Our Lord Jesus the Christ.

We pray thy will be done.

Amen

Experiencing a Healing Moment

Brother often invites us to share a spiritual experience with him at the end of a meditation. The one listed here is a shared healing moment.

The many beings who are gathered around you ask you if you will enjoin together, one with another, all with the loving spirit who fill your planes, and open your beings to light. Accept the healing and the light which is coming into you and without effort simply allow it to flow on when it has done its work.

Let us take just a moment, because the moment is infinite and simply experience this healing.

Why don't you try it after your meditation? It is amazing how powerful it can be.

Chapter 4

Colour

"Embrace the colours and know that they are there to uplift you and provide the means to give you fulfilment upon the Earth."

Introduction

Many healers use colour in their work and different colours always seem to feature strongly in the meditational state. We are used to associating colour with different parts of the body, different emotional states and many 'see' auras as masses of colour.

Following the group's experiences with colour in meditation, Brother was asked to shed further light on the subject. The group found the answers surprising. See what you think.

Turquoise – the Revealing Colour

Stella: I love the colour turquoise but during a meditation I felt very uneasy in it and very isolated. Lynn, too, said that it felt cold and hard. Why was that?

It does not mean that the colour itself is negative. One of its great qualities is to be able to reflect anything within you which reveals your fears and that is a wonderful tool, isn't it? Because it can reveal to you things from within yourself of which you are not aware.

It might be a fear of being alone and isolated. If it is, once you are aware it is there, you will bring it into the light and, as with all fears, when they are brought into the light they are revealed as the little bogeymen that they are and disappear.

Stella: I wasn't aware of holding that fear but I do realise there is a difference between what we fear in the unconscious and what we fear in the conscious state.

Perhaps there is a hidden residue of being out of synchronisation, of not finding your place. It would be buried deep within you, almost not from this life.

The gift of that colour is that it is a **revealing** colour. The secret of it is not to turn back but to walk onwards to face the fear. The feeling you had at that moment was one of being alone and isolated. It was fear of it. If you had walked on, it would have simply fallen away and you would have seen and experienced the overcoming and you would have had a very different feeling about the colour.

The feeling of it being something cold and hard was experienced by one who is warm and feeling. Perhaps, deep within, it is revealing to you the fear of rejection. But rejoice in the revealing because as soon as it is revealed, you walk on through it and it will disappear.

And that is the beauty and the joy of experiencing within that colour vibration, beyond the obvious level of it. You often call it the colour of communication and feeling, and that is true. But it is the deepest feelings that it is revealing and communicating to you.

Just as it found the negative, the fear, to bring out in you, as soon as that fear is acknowledged, faced and overcome it will accentuate the beauty within it, the achievement and, indeed, will open a new door into a higher plane of existence that is open to you **now.** You don't have to wait until you have let go of physical life, it is open to you **now,** as soon as you have walked through, faced and released. It is of great benefit when you understand how to use it.

Using Turquoise

When you encounter a situation where you feel fear or unease, place turquoise, your revealing colour, around yourself and go into the colour. Then, even when you are brought in contact with the feeling of the fear, however you experience it, you will go forward into it. As you go on and merge with it, you will have conquered it and the experience will never be the same again. You will be so changed that never again will you experience that unease, that fear. It is a powerful tool and leads to a wonderful transition.

The Colour Pearl

Lynn: In a meditation I felt that the colour pearl was being poured through me and I felt cleansed. Can you comment on that?

Insights to help you with your daily life are often shown in meditation and this is one.

When you are in a situation within your life where you feel a need of cleansing immerse yourself in the pearl colour. See it being poured through you and around you and you will feel the cleansing and then you will see things very differently. Use this in the little stressful situations of the day.

The Colour Pink

Stella: During a meditation I immersed myself in the colour pink. To my surprise I found that I was quite comfortable in the mid pink (crushed raspberry shade) but I felt little in the beautiful palest rose pink. Why the differences?

That is because you were reacting to the comfortable vibration, because as a denser section of the ray, it is closer to the earth. So, to a physical mind, it is more comfortable. You were able to see and achieve the finest vibration along that particular colour ray, the palest pink, but you could not feel the same degree of comfort.

That will come. You have achieved sensing it but it is shown to you as a new dawning, perhaps. You have achieved the sight of it but you need to overcome some things before you can fully experience it. The turquoise colour will help you to reveal them and, as you walk through releasing them, you will come out into a part where you indeed react to and with that finer vibration. Be glad of the understanding and look forward with anticipation to the next stage of your journey.

The Colour Purple

Stella: We always think of purple as being a very high, fine vibration and yet sometimes we feel comfortable and secure when it is wrapped around us. Why is that?

Because you are loving spirits. Loving spirit, all loving spirit, is wrapped around with the light and will feel its comfort.

Stella: Security mainly.

Yes, because it is the greatest security and yet, most of all, it is love. Union with the divine, that is the message within it.

The only ones who will not feel the comfort of that are ones who shield themselves from the light and they are the ones that are in greatest need. We must all do our best to get light to them.

Earth – the Blue and Green Planet

Stella: In pictures of the Earth taken from space, it is always seen as green and blue. Does this have any significance?

It is not accidental. You often identify green as the meeting place of heaven and earth. You know blue as the first step within the heaven side of the colour spectrum, the spirit consciousness.

Your beautiful planet is there to allow those who are ready to experience the meeting place of heaven and earth, to walk it with spirit and to take those steps in moving the centre of consciousness into the spirit perception, the spirit mind. That is why it is seen as those colours.

Think how wonderful it will be when you are ready to inhabit, to experience, the indigo, the violet, the pure gold and the white light encompassed in them. You see all are wonderful journeys but there is need to overcome challenges to help you reach the greater understanding and awareness needed. Welcome the obstacles because, indeed, they are the means.

Lynn: The opportunity for growth.

Yes. So embrace the colours and know that they are there to uplift you and provide the means to give you fulfilment upon the Earth.

Golden Light

When you learn to go in trust there is no fear.

When you learn to give yourself to the inner union
completely in trust you will soar to the heights. You will
experience the whole breadth of the colour vibrations and
experience the freedom within them. You will find the
golden light.

You might not understand the achievement but instant
understanding isn't always available. Sometimes it is
necessary to discover and experience before understanding
comes. Sometimes it is necessary to go through a barrier
alone, to experience being one with the universe and through
that transition to know true freedom of spirit and the
upliftment of the golden light.

Beauty of our Realm

Thank God for the beauty of our realm, for the joy of sharing
with all we meet and with all life within God.

Thank God for the perceptions and the keys found and the
knowledge that there are other keys and other kingdoms to
conquer; for the knowledge that as we walk forward
shedding fear, in trust, then the beauty of the places where
we walk will show us God in the brightest raiment.

Look and you will see God.
Listen and you will hear God.
Stand and you will feel God, His peace, His love.

Chapter 5

Living and Letting Go

"When you learn to let love, from the greater mind, control thought, then you have truly overcome fear."

Introduction

We are all currently living a physical life. If you are reading these words, that is certain! For my part, it is also true that I sometimes have difficulty in really understanding the relationship between this life and that inner knowledge that I believe we all have of something greater.

Brother often speaks to us of the need to take one step at a time and the impossibility of understanding until we have completed a cycle of discovery and experience. He also tells us that as we reach each point of understanding we discover many other mysteries!

However, he does answer our questions to the limit of our current understanding and this chapter has a selection that has helped us at different times.

Taking on a Physical Life

Brother was asked if he could explain a little to us about what happens when a spirit enters a physical life.

Initially, when a spirit takes on the physical form, for a while it is still much more alive within its spirit consciousness. It has to learn of the physical world. I am not speaking of onlywithin the womb, but of while a little baby.

You see that babies are often asleep and wake to meet physical needs, needs of the body. What do you think is happening during that sleep?

Stella: I think they have popped back home.

They have never left home. None of you ever do leave home. What you leave is the consciousness of the home.

While the baby is learning to accept and respond to earthly sensations and how to register them within this strange little body, it is stepping more and more into the conscious mind until that mind becomes dominant.

It is a gradual process. We can liken it a balance that can only have a particular weight on either side. There is a steady movement of the weights from one side to the other as the baby enters more and more into its new 'reality'.

During that process, a great deal is learnt by fear, for example that fire burns and that some things are unpleasant and to be avoided.

One of the greatest challenges of walking within a physical sphere is learning to respond to fear because much learning from an early age has fear at the root. This is the biggest difference between the spirit mind and the human mind which, having responded to fear from the start, then holds that fear to shape what are then perceived as needs.

How do you define a need? It is something that perhaps you are frightened to be without. Fear is an element in it. Whereas in your spirit mind, the greater mind, you operate without fear.

The challenge, every time this journey is undertaken, is to start altering those weights upon the balance and moving from a mind controlled by fear to a mind controlled by love and trust. That is part of the purpose of physical life – to make the journey from 'fear' control to 'love' control.

What you are doing by various means is changing the weights on the scales and merging these consciousnesses so that fear isn't dominant. Fear doesn't drive you. Fear doesn't guide you. Indeed it has its place. You all know of the mechanisms within you which help you through fearful situations. That is a positive side, but the fear I speak of is the fear which controls thought and thought is part of God's creative power.

When you learn to let love from the greater mind control thought, then you have truly overcome fear.

Sense of Loss at Physical Birth

Lynn: Doesn't everyone feel a sense of abandonment and loss when we come into this world because of the loss of the love that surrounds us in spirit?

Yes indeed, but it is part of the journey. One of the lessons of walking within the physical form is learning that that feeling is, in fact, illusion. Once that lesson has been learned never again will that sense of abandonment be felt.

It may take more than one pathway of life to appreciate that, but what a great empowerment and release when you reach that point of understanding, of total belonging forever and ever. Then you know that anything other than belonging is illusion. In that belonging is all the love, help and understanding we ever need.

You are spirit now as much as you ever were and ever will be. With the understanding of that comes the certain knowledge that you can never be abandoned or cut off from loving spirit.

When the time is right even this will be seen in its rightful context.

Belonging

Stella: Would you say that the greatest fear for human beings is the fear of sickness and dying?

I would suggest that one of the greatest fears is the fear of not belonging. And that is losing sight of the fact that we are always and forever belonging to our spirit family, belonging to God.

How can that fear be overcome? By releasing it and thus being released from the prison that it brings. The fear of being alone, of being isolated, is a prison which stops people from looking into their heaven and seeing that they are part of it, that they belong.

Stella: I think, really, in the end where people think they don't belong they eventually doubt themselves. I wonder then if you start believing in what people are saying about you.

For many that is the case. What I am really trying to show you is that release is a gift. It is such an important lesson because until that particular point of understanding has been found, trust is just a word as well.

It is essential to understand release in order to understand trust because in the power to release is the total acknowledgement of belonging. It brings the knowledge of not being cast adrift, of being empowered, of never being isolated and of having the ability to, finally, let go fear.

The ability to say not 'what if' but 'what is' is a release.

Spirit Spheres Merging

Alastair: I think I was either dreaming or in a meditation and what I saw was like two spheres which I felt were spirits; two different spirits merging that allowed each of them to experience the other person's lives, thoughts and emotions and all their history without being judgemental. Was that something that I imagined or is that something that in the spirit world is actually possible?

It was probable that what you were seeing was different facets of yourself, of your own being. And the coming together and being absorbed, non-judgementally, is how each of the experiences - the learning experiences that you call life - is absorbed into our greater being.

So you were seeing, I believe, an aspect of different parts of yourself coming together and that means you had reached a point of understanding which allowed that merging. It is one of the little markers along the way.

Meditation, and sometimes even dreaming, is opening the way within you.

All the time you speak of climbing up and soaring and other such things. They are just images which are bringing you closer to the true centre of your own beings. There are a lot of other layers still to go.

Release

Stella: Is it necessary to learn how to release ourselves from those things that hold us back?

Release is one of those facets of life which must be learned and can only be learned by the individual because, until it has been fully discovered and experienced and the point of understanding reached, it is just a word without meaning.

Without learning how to release you cannot really fully embrace trust, for release needs to be learned before trust becomes total reality.

Often words are used without a clear perception of their true meaning. You say, "I require peace, send me peace. Dear Father please let me walk in peace." To walk in peace you need to think peace. Do you think it possible that some of the messengers of the Father say to you, "Why are you asking us, you are the only ones who can determine how you think?"

You may say, "I am going to send out love and only love." Then something happens and the intention is forgotten. It may be in reaction, but even a reaction is our own responsibility.

You say, "Dear Father, please let me walk in love." Is it possible that some of the messengers of the Father who come to help you say, "Why are you asking because you are the only ones that can achieve walking in love?"

Of course, no messenger of love would say that to you. Help is always given but the truth remains that it is the responsibility of each individual to embrace the chosen pathways. It is part of God's divine trust in us that He releases us to find our way. He allows us to learn, to experience and to walk forward into the ultimate release, the release of personality.

That idea may seem difficult for you at this time and yet you do not find it hard to embrace the idea that you have been, perhaps, different personalities in different physical lives.

Stella: We accept the idea of re-incarnation meaning that we have had different physical identities but are we different personalities? Surely we are just facets of our spiritual self.

So the question arises, does the personality belong to the spirit self or is the personality a part of the facet?

It can be many different things. We have spoken before of the possibility that revered names and despised names within the Earth's history could well be the same spirit. You might say different personalities or just different facets of the same personality.

Perhaps the latter is nearer the truth because we are all on journeys to discover the way of balance and to discover our true natures and the nature of God. In order to do this we would need to experience life from many different perspectives. Perhaps it is a perspective of the personality that is prominent at each stage and it is that perspective that we need to release as we progress.

However we may choose to express it, it is undeniable that to fully experience something we first need to let it go. Release, as God releases us to find our way. That does not mean He casts us out or cuts us off. Nor does it mean He makes us walk without help. It means He holds us in such love and trust and gives us time to find our own way.

Free Will

Stella: *Is it possible through our own choice to avoid whatever was the purpose of the physical pathway?*

Yes, it is. Free will is absolute. It can happen when the conscious mind is overpowering. The more you are able to access your controlling spirit mind, however, the less likely this is.

However, if it does happen, the time will come, when there is realisation that a purpose of a life pathway had not been achieved. With the benefit of their new understanding the individual spirit would ask for the opportunity to walk another physical pathway in order to achieve it. Not because they have to, but because they have reached a point where they choose to. Free will again, you see.

Free will is God's great gift to us. It is through this gift that we grow in understanding and learn to walk in trust.

Letting Go

This is a dialogue about letting go of old hurts.

Stella: Brother, are you ever really sure that you have got rid of all the old hang-ups? I think I have but sometimes things that I thought I had got rid of years ago have come back. So I pushed them out again but ...

Do not push them out. Pull them in. Face them and ensure that every part is thought through and sorted out.

Can we ever be really sure? We can only be sure according to our current understanding and our understanding is constantly changing. Therefore sometimes you can quite truthfully say that something is dealt with. It is not an issue any more.

Stella: You know, an hour ago I could have sworn that I had offloaded all the old rubbish but now I am not sure.

That shows you that your capacity has grown in that hour. The light comes in according to your capacity, thus revealing other aspects to you. Be glad of that. Do not push the new thoughts away. Bring them into focus.

Lynn: Expose them

Yes, indeed, but remember all of them have gone. The lessons only remain.

Stella: Yes, as long as we have taken the lessons.

Perhaps there are some other lessons within them.

Stella: Is that why they come back?

Yes. You have taken the lessons that were available to you according to your previous capacity. Your capacity is growing constantly so the incidents that hold further lessons for you come back. But remember, it is the lesson only that comes back. Do not attempt to judge yourselves because you cannot. Whatever the actions were, they were taken from a capacity which has long gone. Do you understand?

Stella: Yes. Years ago you thought you were right. Now, you can look back and think, 'no, that wasn't right', but you didn't have that capacity then.

Yes. Do not make it an exercise of blame. Simply look for the additional lessons and take them and then bless and release.

Lynn: I was going to say we should bless them, because we did the best we could with what we knew at that time.

Stella: Whatever decision we made on the whole we made what we thought was right. I know that is not always true but I think generally the main part is based on a feeling of truth.

From where you stand at the time you make the decision that you think is best for you. But as you change you sometimes realise that what seemed important was, indeed, vastly unimportant. Real nuggets of truth and of importance, were lying there waiting to be seen like little diamonds within a seam of rock. Overlooked, sometimes for many years, but waiting there to be perceived.

When these things from the past come back to you, they come back because your understanding has changed and it is time to see another diamond.

So rejoice in that. Take the diamond and just let the rest go.

Our Controlling Spirit Reality

Brother continually reminds us that we are spirit now, even while we are in a physical form. Here he explains a little more to us about our controlling spirit reality.

Within your bodies you know there is a system which works to maintain the equilibrium of your being without conscious effort.

Lynn: The autonomic nervous system.

That is right. It keeps the blood flowing, the heart beating.

Stella: Breathing even when you are asleep.

You have just such a system working within your greater mind, powered from spirit, working in spirit, but also working even within that part of spirit which is manifest for a short time within your physical form.

It is guarding, preserving, maintaining, giving energy, giving peace, giving warning and giving comfort when it is needed. It opens pathways to allow loving beings to come together. It creates the means to allow the flow of energy triggered by prayer to flow through all life.

It is as real as the system within your physical bodies.

It is part of God's great creation.

You are spirit now. You always were and you always will be.

Listen

Listen - what do you hear?
In the silence all around you, what do you hear?

Look - what do you see?
Look into the void, into the distances, what do you see?

Reach out - what do you touch?

What do you feel when you touch the earth?
What do you feel when you touch the skies?
What do you feel when you touch the seas?
What do you feel when you touch a heartbeat?

You hear me in the silence.
You see me in the void.
You feel me in the touch, for I am always there.
I am in God, and God is within you.
Listen and you will hear Him.

When there is no voice, you still hear God.
When there is no form, you still see God.
When there is no substance, you still touch God.
For God is all around you. God is in you.
You are part of God.

Listen - and you WILL hear.

Chapter 6

Balance, Light and Change

"**You** have the answer to your prayers within you and **you** have that within you that can heal and repair, uplift and create, that allows you to walk in light and to perceive and experience the **I AM**."

Introduction

We are often urged to seek the way of balance. People talk of imbalances causing problems in many different aspects of life. It is a concept that is used a great deal when speaking of spiritual development and awareness.

We also speak of going into the light or opening to the light.

This chapter looks at different aspects and perceptions of balance and light. This necessarily embraces another, often difficult, concept for us – that of change. As always we are advised to step back and look at ourselves objectively and learn to recognise our different perceptions of those things around us.

Balance

A question was asked, "What is balance?"

I would say God is balance. I would say God not only holds the balance of the universe, of all life, of every thread within it but God **is** the balance.

You might then say, "How can anything ever be out of balance then because God is in all life? God is supreme light, love, so how can there ever be such a thing as imbalance?"

In the total scheme of things I believe that is true. However along the way there are many perceptions of imbalance just as there are many perceptions of life. Of course, you can only define balance from your point of perception. That definition will be true only for an instant. By the time it is formulated it will already be no longer valid.

You think now of the life form you are in as whole and complete. Yet when you are fully operating once more from within your spirit self you will perceive that physical life as one little facet of a whole just as your little finger is a part of your body.

Indeed, it is possible that you may perceive several physical lives as facets of yourself and forget the idea of linear time from within a spirit perception. You may see these different parts of lives, not only physical lives but other areas that once seemed so real, as the learning opportunities that they are with your whole and complete being very capable of undertaking more than one at a time.

Remember God entrusts to each one the spark of God. God entrusts to each one the opportunity to come, by his/her own efforts, choices and decisions, into the full flower of the Godness.

As sparks of God united in God there must be total balance and, indeed, had we not the balance of God that wonderful balance of life could not be achieved and perpetuated. But in the individual quest to come into the full knowledge and flower of the Godness, the perceptions of imbalance are so very real. God entrusts us in love and wisdom to fully come into our rightful place and never forget that the living God light, the God spark, is in everyone.

The Living Entity of Light

Lynn: Why do you speak of the light as 'living'?

The light is indeed a *living* entity. From where do you think this light comes? From God you might say, but how is God's light manifest? It is through God's beings. So, what is the light but the generated light from each one because the beings of God come through the darkness into the light. In their growing understanding of their nature and the nature of God, comes the generation of the light and the light is unifying.

I hear you sometimes saying, *my* light, *your* light, *God's* light, *that* light. It is just light, it is one. Light is one but it comes from **each** one. Indeed it is a living and a changing entity but light itself does not change. The entity of the light is dynamic because it is being added to.

As you go through each door into a greater generation and understanding of the living entity of light, you carry a greater responsibility. From your deeper knowledge, from your flowering of loving spirit you cannot go back. You cannot reach a point where you say "but it was quite comfortable to do whatever I wanted and to ignore everybody else" and then try to recapture it.

Oh yes, it is a stage everyone has to go through because we have to learn to make the right decisions not simply for a perceived physical personality but for the true personality, the child of God. Once touched by the light, you walk with that greater responsibility with you in all the little decisions of the day, in all the big decisions of the spirit and in every one in between.

Rejoice at the growth. Rejoice at the greater understanding and what a wonderful step forward to perceive that much more of the reality of God's Universe – to know that all things within it are living and dynamic. All are changeless and changing. All come from within each and every being. Yes, each one of us has a responsibility to every other living being to generate the light, to provide it, to create the material that will keep the darkness out; to create the power that will be used for healing, for repair, wherever it is necessary. You start by praying to a distant God to provide. As you go along your journeys you realise that you are part of the provision. **You** are providers. **You** have the answer to your prayers within you and **you** have that within you that can heal and repair, uplift and create, that allows you to walk in light and to perceive and experience the **I AM**.

The Inner Pathway of Light

Stella: Sometimes, in meditation, we touch what you call the Inner Pathway of Light. How can we find that pathway in our day to day lives and share it with others?

The entrance to the way of light is within you. It is within every being. When you discover the beauty and the joy of that light you wish to share it with other people. Once you have discovered it, you become carriers of the light, containers for the light.

Every time you pray for others, send thanks to God or by a kind word, thought or deed you do something to help your fellow creation, God's light within you grows and reaches out. It is not confined by any barrier of your being or of the physical world, because it is of spirit and you are fully and wholly spirit now, even while you are in physical form. Every other being is also spirit now. So when the light

65

shines out unconfined in limitless spirit it touches every other spirit life.

However, each individual must open to allow it into their own physical consciousness. That is a journey that everyone must undertake for themselves. It is a journey in understanding but you can open to the light without understanding the process. Indeed a loving heart is all that is needed.

Love is the key that opens the inner door, revealing the pathway of infinite and powerful light. Where does that pathway take you? It takes you into the consciousness and reality of your true spirit selves. It changes you for evermore.

Coming into Wholeness

Lynn: Sometimes it is hard to see the spark of God in ourselves let alone on others. Can you help us with that?

Only together do we come to wholeness and yet, individually, one of God's great gifts is to allow us to find our way. Just as every other person we see or meet is exercising the right to find their way, to allow their own God light to shine.

Everyone has a unique gift to bring to the world, whether we perceive it or not. Everyone is a truly loved child of God, existing within God's family.

Some of the times which seem so tempestuous and the challenges which seem so hard are simply necessary steps and challenges to help bring you and all others into the knowledge of their true beings, to achieve the shining light of God.

Truth

Brother often speaks about truth and the perception of truth.

Stella: Don't you find that we have different layers of truth on Earth?

No, you have different understandings of truth. Your understanding changes as you change and grow. It is very often thought that truth is absolute and the same for everyone.

Stella: No it isn't.

Perhaps it is, but their perception of it is not.

One of the lessons that comes from the physical pathways is the importance of truth. But within the physical sphere, you walk through the mists of untruth all the time.

There are a few fundamental truths.

God is a fundamental truth.

God is love.

We are all existing in God. The spark of God is within us.

Love is a fundamental truth.

Life is a fundamental truth.

Often, other things that you think of as truth are really a matter of perception. As you go through your lives your 'truths' change, don't they? As children your truth might have been that God created the world in six days. As you learn more of life and of the nature of life, you realise that is simply an illusory way of expressing creation. It did not make it a lie, did it? It was a truth of the time. At the time it was written it was a perception of truth.

Your understanding of what the universe is at present is a truth to you, even though you are aware that there is so much you do not see and understand.

Your perception of a 'truth' changes. Within the physical sphere there is so much which isn't even an expression of the current perception of truth. There is so much self deceit.

There is a need for a greater perception of the truth to be embraced as preparation for the new light to be received. Light comes through individuals and when there is sufficient of it, it changes the world.

The change is possible. It is important that you embrace and realise that truth. The change is in your hands and in the hands of every other being. But you cannot act for anyone else, only for yourselves.

Your responsibility, if you open to receive this light, is to let your light shine out. If you do that, the light in your world will unite with other lights until it is sufficient to banish the darkness of deceit and allow you to open in preparation for the even greater light of Christ to come. And with it, the understanding of 'truth'.

Change in Every Moment

Stella: Why is that when you reach a new understanding of something it often feels like you have really known it for ages? It seems so obvious and natural.

That is because every little change is natural to the moment. It is the moment that changes and, in every moment, you change and your world changes, your knowledge of your true selves and God's realm changes and your experience and your understanding changes. But every change is natural to the moment.

Lack and Abundance

Stella: The concept of freedom is sometimes hard to equate with the concept of constraint. Can you help us with that?

It is a simple truth that we learn the understanding of freedom through experiencing constraint. The only way you can learn freedom is to experience the lack of it.

In the perfection of God's realm where everyone has the consciousness of their oneness in God, how can anyone know how great that gift is? How can we know? We only know by experiencing, one part at a time, constraint and then learning that the constraint is an illusion. For at no one moment do you ever leave that unity within God. All you are doing is experiencing within a limited consciousness. What you call your physical consciousness is but one tiny part of your real self, one tiny part of your potential.

Experiencing constraint enables you to find your way out from it through choice. It enables you to understand every single part and element of lack in order to fully rejoice in the beauty and wonder of abundance.

Sometimes in meditation, you reach a point that is so wonderful that you don't want to leave it but you know you have to. That is when you touch your spirit consciousness and experience once more what life really is. That is the reality that you never leave. The lack, the constraint is the illusion that will fall away from you as soon as you allow it to. It is part of the mystery that when you are in constraint and the sense of lack, you cling to it for fear that what it outside of it is worse.

It is helping you to learn the real meaning of that wonderful word 'trust', of learning to give your trust to God as God gives His trust to you. Learning to trust what God trusts is learning to trust yourselves. Each one of you is worthy of trust. Each one of you, as you walk in trust, will experience more and more of the true and loving reality of your true spirit, which is **now**. Never do you leave it. Never are you closed off from it and, through that reality, never are you outside of that loving and supporting circle of spirit which is always with you.

If you could learn to view through those eyes which always see, the world around you would seem a very different place.

Know Yourself

Know yourself - and you will know God.
For God is within you. He is part of you, as He is part of all
creation.

In God, you share in creation. You are part of all that has
gone before - all that is yet to be.

You are part of the mountains, of the seas, of
the sky, of the universe, of the universes yet unseen.

You are part of the trees, part of the flowers,
part of creation, part of God.

Only you can fulfil your purpose.
All of creation is dependent on you, as you are dependent on all
creation.

Look within you and you will find God.
The answer to all your questions is within you,
the object of your quest - that which you are seeking -
within you, part of you.

Know yourself - and you will know God.

Light in the Darkness

Thank God for the light offered to us. Walk forward to the greater light beckoning. Ask that you may see the way to make the right decisions to open the pathways of love and light and service, that each one will fulfil their purpose and grow even closer together within the beauty of that love.

Send that light to those in the darkness of despair, in need, in the blindness which is so much worse than physical blindness, those who remain blind to the greater realm around them.

Walk in trust and know that you are trusted.

Chapter 7

The Tempter Within

"The tempter within will **magnify your fears** and so give you the opportunity to face them and deal with them. Those fears will only be revealed when you are in a position to overcome them."

Introduction

Sometimes, Brother refers to 'the tempter within', which he tells us is a much misunderstood concept. He says it is lack of understanding that has given rise to the idea of the devil as a separate entity, outside of our own beings just as God has been portrayed for centuries as a separate entity. These questions all concern our understanding of this concept.

Does the Devil Exist?

Stella: Does the devil exist?

The idea of the devil has existed from the earliest times. Originally, the devil was portrayed as a serpent, a being separate from man, but that portrayal showed a lack of understanding by the ones who recorded the words. The words were passed down and the lack of understanding was compounded in the chain of their passing. The 'devil' was not a separate entity but 'the tempter within', actually part of everyone as God is part of everyone.

The Temptation of Jesus

Think, too, of the words that were written about the tempting of the Master Jesus. It is written that he stood at the top of a great height and the devil, the tempter, was standing there with him. The devil said, 'If you are son of God jump because you will not be hurt.'

The Master Jesus knew that it was the tempter within. It was the ones who wrote the words who could not grasp that fact. They could only make sense of them if it was a conversation with somebody outside of self. But there was no pretence by the Master. It was a lack of understanding as the words were written and a lack of perception of the true meaning of those words by so many since that has given rise to centuries of fear - fear of hell fire, fear of eternal damnation and fear that there is one waiting to lead you to them.

Lynn: What was being shown to Jesus in that temptation?

When that tempting was taking place, it was at a period where there was great acclaim for the pathway that the Master Jesus was walking. There had been many healings and many other things labelled 'miracles', even though they were according to the great natural law of life but a law that was not – and still is not – fully understood. Many people were aware of his shining spirit, his holiness which, for some, was a challenge. To others He became a figure of acclaim and that picture they held of him in their minds was false, too. He was called the only-begotten Son of God, the King of Heaven. So the 'tempter within' said to him, 'You are Son of God - jump off this precipice, you can't be hurt because you are the Son of God. How could the Son of God be hurt? Normal laws don't apply to you. You're different from us.'

In that instance, the 'tempter within' was saying, 'Go on, ignore the natural law of the physical world in which you live because you are above that natural law'. But the Master Jesus forever said, 'I am son of man, we are all children of the Father'.

When the Master Jesus told those around Him of the inner temptation, the words were passed from one to another without the true understanding, so it came to be relayed as if there was someone standing beside Him, who was doing the tempting.

And the words remain there waiting to be understood by everyone in their own time. The words are still true but the temptation was by the 'tempter within'.

Indeed the Master Jesus walked a pathway as man with the same challenges that we all have, overcoming fear even though the fear was of a different form.

In the garden of Gethsemane, did He not say 'Father, take this away'? And had He really meant it, it would have been taken away.

It was the moment of fear, the 'tempter within' again, but the challenge was faced within that garden and the challenge was overcome. The Master Jesus walked on in the knowledge that this was His chosen pathway and He chose to complete it. He had to be truly man, truly having to face the challenges as we do, each one of us, but in different forms.

Concepts of Heaven and Hell

Lynn: Why was the devil originally portrayed as a serpent?

At the time, the greatest symbol of fear was the serpent so that was the personification put upon 'the tempter within'.

Lynn: How does this affect the concepts of heaven and hell?

The illusion that has been perpetrated is that there is on the one side this place called 'heaven', for those who do good, and on the other this place called 'hell', place of suffering and misery for those who do evil. They are both physical concepts. They can have no meaning whatsoever within the understanding of the spirit.

We should remember that God is love. In God WE ARE. In God I AM. I AM even though I carry within me my own heaven and my own hell.

One of the greatest tools for growth and understanding given to each of us is this concept of the tempter. The 'tempter within' will show us our weaknesses. It will present us continually with challenges. It will say to us, 'Why do you let that one treat you like that? They are not treating you properly.'

The tempter within will **magnify your fears** and so give you the opportunity to face them and deal with them. Those fears will only be revealed when you are in a position to overcome them.

Stella: Why is it that such graphic and fearful depictions of the devil and hell proliferate in literature and sacred writings?

Forget the words like 'devil' and ideas of places of eternal damnation. Of course there could be no such thing. Forget the misunderstandings that have led to words being written in good faith which are just words written from a lack of vision. At the time, they were the clearest images and explanations the writer could find from within a limited understanding. New understandings are continually being reached. If you review those instances in the literatures of the faiths of the world with your current knowledge that the 'tempter' is the 'tempter within', a friend to help show you the next step on the way, you will see them very differently.

Use the tempter as a friend and know that it is part of you. Look at the little temptations and try to see them, not in just the most obvious light, but in a light of loving expectancy that they will reveal to you something about yourself that you had not previously been aware of.

You carry heaven and hell within you, part of you, therefore part of God. You are seeking always the way of balance, balancing those ideas until they merge into one because indeed they are the two sides of the same thing. When I say use the tempter as a friend, I mean that quite literally.

How Can Temptations Help Us?

Stella: Many people now seem to be suffering from depression and low self-esteem. Can this be attributed to the 'tempter within'?

There are many people who are put into the little box labelled 'suffering from depression' and there are many different causes.

Some have difficulty coping with life and perhaps that is their tempter saying to them, 'Others can do that but you can't', or, 'you are not worthy of that'.

With others the 'tempter within' says to them, 'You should be ahead of everyone else, you should be recognised as such, you should be outperforming everyone else.'

In every case, the 'tempter within' is revealing a challenge and, when that happens, it is certain that the means to overcome is within the individual's grasp. You need to look beyond the obvious because sometimes things come in a form that you would not think of as a temptation. Perhaps it is revealing the fear of not achieving and not always being the first in every field. The overcoming is in the acceptance that there are times and fields where one will excel and others where one will not.

Many problems are caused by carrying unreasonable expectations. When they cannot be met, instead of looking again at the whole thing and accepting, there is often an anger that is turned on other people. It must be somebody else's fault when in fact blame should not come into it at all. There should be no judgement, no blame, just learning. They are not recognising their great friend, 'the tempter within', and not dealing with the challenge which has been brought to them, which they have earned and which they are able to overcome.

The tempter within is part of us, therefore part of God.

The Root of Fear

Lynn: Is the tempter within part of our physical being only or part of our spirit self?

It is part of your true being and continues until the perfect point of balance and understanding is reached, which we call perfection, whatever perfection may be. I do not pretend to know it. It is part of our true being in spirit.

The tempter within takes a different form in your spiritual and your physical consciousnesses because the challenges are different. It is a tool only, not a separate being, not a personality, part of YOU, a tool to reveal to you your deepest fears and your challenges.

Lynn: Would those challenges happen together? Could the fears people might experience be the fears from spirit and fears from the physical? Could it be multi-faceted?

Indeed yes, but not exactly in the way that you are asking the question. You are spirit the whole time. You are not two separate beings; you are not **you** the physical and **you** the spirit. Even though **you** the physical bears one name that is superfluous within the spirit.

Lynn: So I think what my question probably should have been is 'do we have fears that we actually create from the physical life that we are living and then fears that we bring from the spirit?'

The fears are within the **true you**. Fear comes from within the true you. The manifestation of that fear is expressed through your physical consciousness while you are experiencing within a physical domain. For example, some people have a fear of spiders, which is a physical thing. But the basis of that fear comes from a different form within the true centre of your being and finds a way of manifesting itself in a physical form.

Lynn: So really what we are saying is, there can be a fear that is held within the spiritual consciousness that we can enhance or diminish in our physical consciousness.

Indeed, yes. For many, the reason for undertaking a physical existence is to deal with a fear. Sometimes, the physical manifestation of it is easier to recognise and deal with than the fear in another form.

Partly the problem is, that many beings within a physical consciousness hold onto the idea that there is a life in spirit which is left behind during a life on Earth, and, when the time is right, the physical life is left behind and life in spirit resumed.

But you are spirit the whole time. The only true life is that ongoing life in spirit, the 'I AM'. You cannot say the 'I AM' is the physical being. The physical being is born and changes and dies. The true reality of life, the spirit which is the 'I AM', always **is**, even while the awareness can be confined into small channels, as it were, for specific reasons of experience. Your physical lives are just such channels even though they seem whole and complete while you are within them.

And yet many people reach the stage of awareness in which the physical life does not seem whole any more. They reach the stage where they have complete and absolute certainty that their true reality is the spirit self.

Stella: And sometimes we are lucky enough to be absorbed in that feeling that we are totally cared for, totally loved and yet totally self responsible - which we know we are all the time - but with the ability to move forward. When I am there I know that I am completely within my spirit self.

Your spirit consciousness, rather, because you are spirit all the time. You experience that total belonging with your spirit family. You experience it as fully as if you did not have a physical image. You do not suspect it, you know it.

Challenges and Fear

Lynn: Why is it that every challenge seems to be to do with fear in some way?

It has been said that the purpose of walking within a physical awareness is to learn to overcome fear. The 'tempter within' is a mighty tool to help reveal to you fear because, as I have said, some fears are not always obvious. But the 'tempter within' will always uncover the fear for you and show you the lessons you need to learn.

The 'tempter within', which is part of you, is for you and you alone. When that perfect balance is reached it will be part of the YOU in the total knowledge and awareness of your place in God, your Godness. The 'tempter within' is indeed a mighty, powerful, valuable and useful tool.

With the true understanding of this there comes a breakthrough, a breakthrough in your understanding of yourselves and of others. So often, behaviour which you find hard to understand is the result of an individual who is reacting to the 'tempter within' without, yet, finding the proper understanding.

As you know, negative action from one often elicits negative reaction in another.

So take the knowledge with you into your daily lives and you will find that with it comes the means to disperse passion, to overcome anger and to stop the endless chain of action and reaction which leads to so much discord within the world. You see now how you can stop these cycles that bring darkness to so many lives? There are so many situations where you react from fear. The 'tempter within', by showing you the fear, gives you the means to recognise it and deal with it.

It comes through from your true being, into your mind and is manifest within your bodies.

You cannot separate the parts. What **is** in one part **is** within the whole. Yet so many illnesses, many of them very serious ones, have fear at their root. It is recognised that many of them are caused by that physical word 'STRESS' which is a manifestation of fear.

How much easier it will be to deal with them now that you understand that it is your friend, the 'tempter within', showing you the little problem to be overcome with the sure and certain knowledge that you have the means to overcome it. If you accept the problem and do not try to push blame onto anybody else, it will be easy to do something about it. Then the stress and, with it, the illness goes.

Lynn: Don't we sometimes try to overcome the fear and then the danger is that we go too far the other way, into ego?

That is right and then your great friend, the 'tempter within', comes to your rescue with another temptation. It is always there for you to show you the different sides of everything until eventually a line of balance is found.

Give thanks for the knowledge and use the 'tempter within' as your friend.

Little Mysteries

All of life, all of the greater life too, is made up of little mysteries. Take one step at a time and soon there is one mystery less. Then when you look back, you will realise you have solved some very big mysteries but you did it one step at a time, one little mystery at a time. And that is the way through everything.

It is God's way, but everyone takes their own steps. No-one can do it for you.

Simple Truth

Thank God for the light of understanding, for the touch of healing, for the knowledge of deep peace within us. Thank God for His hand supporting and balancing our world. Know that, through God, each one may be a true channel of light, a true channel of peace, of harmony and of healing that can change the world. Believe it, for it is simple truth.

Challenge and Experience

There is no bad way, just experience and every experience you take on willingly because you are ready for the challenge. And every one you take on you have the ability to overcome. Enjoy the moment. Enjoy the learning.

Chapter 8

Advice for Living

"The little things of the day which you so often take for granted are the lasting ones, the true importance in life. Look to the little things and remember the keys to the kingdom are within you."

Introduction

In our many talks with Brother, questions are often asked about things that are happening around us. Although he says that we must make our own decisions he often gives us some general help. Indeed, Brother says he could not harm us and to attempt to tell us specifically what to do in any situation would deprive us of our challenge which we have earned the right to face and overcome.

Many years ago he was asked how we would know if we were pursuing a 'wrong' path. He often refers to the advice he gave us then which we call 'the pebbles, the rocks, the boulder and the mountain.' He said that at the start the way would be easy, then it would feel as if there were pebbles across the path. It would be quite easy to walk over them but we would notice a little discomfort. Then, further along, we would find rocks in the way. It would take a little more effort to get past these but would still be easily done. Then we would find a big boulder in front of us that would cause real effort to get over or round but we could still do it. After that we would find ourselves right up against a mighty mountain with no pathways over or around it. We could stay there trying to push the mountain out of the way for as long as we wanted to, until we finally discovered that we couldn't do it and had to retrace our steps and find another pathway.

After coming against a mountain for a few times, we would learn to turn back at the boulder, then at the rocks and finally we would recognise our 'mistake' and turn back at the pebbles.

This has helped us enormously. The questions in this chapter are other snippets of advice.

Unkindness

Lynn: Why does there sometimes seem to be so much cruelty and unkindness in the world?

Yes, there are unkind things that happen, but there is so much love in this place of learning. Often when someone or something appears to you as a darkness in your life it is someone giving you a service by offering you a challenge. When you have faced it and you react in love not in anger or hatred, then there will be no need for that challenge to be continued or repeated. You will have reached a new point of understanding.

Lynn: An opportunity for growth.

Everything is an opportunity for growth but all created by God, even though some of the actions are fashioned by man. Therefore, of course there is cruelty. It is man's understanding and perception which needs to learn to see it and to appreciate the learning opportunity, then to use love to create the circumstances where it is no longer necessary. That is an overcoming and each overcoming is a blossom in spirit. Each overcoming is a little acorn found within spirit from which the mighty bright and shining oak tree grows.

Every time you are in a situation where you feel you are under attack, all you do is step into the objective view and you will be amazed at the difference that it makes. See from your spirit eyes.

The time will come when you are operating fully from within your spirit selves. It can happen while you are upon the Earth plane but most times it does not. But when you are operating fully from within that spirit self perspective and you look back at your Earthly pathway, the things that you identify as really important may be the ones that you dismiss as being trivial now.

The little things of the day which you so often take for granted are the lasting ones, the true importance in life. Look to the little things and remember the keys to the kingdom are within you. There is no need to go out and conquer in the material sense. In fact, the going out and conquering is the thing that will appear to be trivial when you have fully resumed your true perception. Then you will see your world as part of God's universe, fulfilling its purpose and perceiving it with love.

When to say No

Stella asked Brother about a situation where people come to her for healing and help. She tries to assist them but, on occasion, she feels it can cause a dependency that is not helpful to them.

What you are really asking is when does help become hindrance?

Stella: That's it. Do we stop them expanding their own mind by saying have you considered this, that and the other.

That is part of the learning and, in it, they are of service to you because it is something that each one has to learn. There will not be a flashing light saying do this, or don't do that because we are all on a unique pathway of learning. While you are working at healing in whichever way that healing is done and you are attuned to your channel of healing you will **know** what is the right action and you will have no doubt.

The doubt comes in afterwards when you are thinking and talking about it.

Learn to trust your channel. The channels are built gradually and those links are not forged within your physical life alone.

Stella: I can believe that because for me I have such total trust in my channels it would not be something that would be natural to come in one lifetime.

But that trust had to be learned.

When you are totally within it, you **know**. The trouble is sometimes when you are perhaps not actually doing the work, but thinking about it, your physical mind becomes dominant and one of the aspects of physical life is the confining, the putting down...

Stella: The little boxes! (Note: Brother has often spoken of us putting everything into little boxes.)

Little boxes, yes, but I was not even thinking of those at the moment. More, the human mind's capacity to place obstacles, to doubt, to look on the negative side, to start saying 'was I right to do that?' There is nothing wrong with that. It is part of your growing. But part of the Earthly pathway is to learn to overcome. And each one of those people that you speak of are helping you learn to overcome. You are helping them with many different things, with healing, with advice and a listening ear, and sometimes with a challenge to them. Sometimes by saying to them "I have given you what it is you need from me, you need to look into yourself now", you are presenting them with a challenge. It will not always be understood or appreciated. Sometimes you are confronted with a situation where you have to say this far, no further.

Stella: We have been there, Brother.

Lynn: Sometimes when you carry people they don't learn to walk.

No, but how they deal with it is not your responsibility. It is part of their learning and, remember, they are never learning alone any more than you are. And perhaps the little jolt was something that they were brought to you to get. Just as others have acted in that capacity for you.

Stella: It is sometimes very hard when most human beings want to be well thought of or liked or something like that and in some situations, we lose the guts to stand up and be counted. That is a failing on our part.

Yes that is right

Stella: But you should be able to stand and say, ' look this is as far as we go, you have to now turn a different way and start being responsible for self.' But it is not easy to do.

Lynn: But it is knowing that point, isn't it?

And you cannot know. That is part of the physical pathway - walking without knowing but walking in trust and in the knowledge that you are never alone.

The Wilderness Time

Stella asked Brother about a time when, because of work pressures, spiritual growth and service appeared to halt.

The Master Jesus, at the height of his acclaim, had the need to walk away from all of the people clamouring for him and seeking healing. He went into the wilderness for 40 days and 40 nights. It was a necessary preparation time. During that time he stopped healing and teaching. He walked away because there was need for a 'wilderness time'.

We all need such times at different stages of our lives, times for recharging and rebalancing. Perhaps a time to fully understand what it is that we have experienced. Sometimes growth has been so great in one area that it has almost confused us with its wonder. Also, when you have achieved a certain level of progress, there is need for a 'testing time'. Part of the real test is to go into the unknown. It would not help to say to you in advance, "for the next period, this is what is going to happen and this is what we want you to overcome and this is what we want you to experience." Part of the challenge and the overcoming involves going into the unknown in trust. There is a need sometimes to dive into the deep and dark pool in order to emerge into the greater light of understanding on the other side.

Only then will you see that you could not have progressed on your pathways of spiritual awareness and service without the experience. You emerge stronger, more secure in your knowledge of self, in your beliefs, in greater certainty of those spirit beings who unite with you and with a new focus. By experiencing a time that is not quite so comfortable, you realise that by clinging to a comfortable existence that has served its purpose, you are in fact stopping growth.

Predetermination and Free Will

Lynn: Is it possible that sometimes spirit need to bring people together to achieve something predetermined?

Sometimes, if it is part of the agreed pathways, it is essential that some people come together for a common purpose. Then, the spirit within will work to create the circumstances to bring individuals together, but even in that you have free will. You must still choose to come together.

The physical plane is merely a servant, there to provide the learning experience. It may appear complicated upon the Earth but it is just so simple within spirit.

What is more natural than that the underlying purpose of your being within the spirit - your higher self - will create the circumstances to enable the union to take place?

It cannot be enforced. It can merely create the circumstance and the choice of action is, as always, with the individual. At different times on a life pathway the individual will find the physical mind in greater control than the spirit one.

At the moment of recognition of the desire of the higher mind, the power of the physical mind is harnessed to discover how to allow the spirit mind's conviction to be integrated into the daily life. You see there are many purposes on every pathway.

God's Divine Law of Justice

Stella: There are people in our history who are seen as evil because they have undoubtedly been responsible for evil actions, sometimes, on a very large scale. If you are what we call an evil monster, do you actually come to realise somewhere along the way that perhaps you ought to question what you are doing or do you just go on believing totally that you are right? If they really believe it is the right thing to do, is it the right action for them at that time?

Everyone when they make a decision makes the one that they believe is the most beneficial for them at that time – note that I say 'beneficial' not 'right' - but they may be holding themselves within a 'prison', within the darkness.

Every individual makes decisions because they have free will. With that free will, each one of us can make the decisions which lead us into a circle of darkness so, then, we make our next decisions from inside that darkness. Remember, we need to experience and choose the path of right. We cannot do that if we have never experienced the darker side.

Even if the decision taken is the one that, for them, appears to be most beneficial at the time, they must still be subject to the laws of the universe. There is no choice in that. As you sow, so you reap. Even though they considered it the best action at the time, if it is a harmful action, then they will reap a future that has been forged by that action.

But this is said without blame. It is a simple fact. As simple as you turn a switch upwards and a light comes on. You do not say, 'Ah the light is on that is good, the light is off that is bad'. It is just a fact. You are still looking at those decisions with judgement and with blame.

A part of the answer to your question is that it is our decision making process and the law of creation that as we sow so we reap, that brings us into understanding. We can walk as far down that pathway of pebbles and rocks and boulders and mountains as we choose. We can hit our heads up against that solid mountain as many times as we like to before we turn round and take a different way. And that is the start of understanding.

Even if an action which has hurt others has been taken from a mistaken belief that it is right, there is still responsibility. I say this without blame. Also, it is a fact that, according to the law of the universe, when the 'right' way is finally seen there must necessarily be an unwinding, a walking back, a revisiting but a revisiting from a different point of understanding.

That is where the phrase comes from that has been so misunderstood, "There will be a gnashing of the teeth." It was interpreted as a place of torment called Hell, but it is just a simple fact, much as the switching of that light on and off.

There must be compassion for the ones who have walked through that pathway and have now discovered a way of light. Can you think how hard it is for each one of us to revisit things that we did before we found the present pathway?

Perhaps for some things that we do now without realising the harm they do, the time will come when we have to view what we have done and surely the tears will flow. But that is part of our learning.

Just as each individual evolves, grows and develops so a race evolves and the world evolves. In a way that is a reflection of God's universe because each one of us is individual and complete and yet we only have true completeness within the unity of God.

It is just that from the physical aspect you cannot always see. And yet it is also true that things are done with the best of intentions which are not really the most helpful things. Know that rising above them, discovering even that this way is wrong, is part of growth.

Send your thoughts and prayers for all who struggle on this pathway. There are many to take them to the right places.

Children who are Psychic

Lynn: There seem to be a greater number of psychically aware children being born into the world. Many are not understood and become quite frightened and it doesn't seem that there is anywhere for them to turn. Can we help them?

There is always a way of help and the way of help is love and prayer.

Stella: That problem is not new is it? Psychic children have been misunderstood through the years and have been accused of being possessed or something similar.

You are right. In your history so much misunderstanding has arisen regarding the ones on this wonderful pathway of love and service, leading to acts of cruelty and isolation. That has happened because of fear and that fear still exists even though many have a greater understanding. It is especially hard for children who are developing their channels.

Those being born with a greater ability to make those spirit links are even more open to receiving your and our thoughts of love and prayers for protection and wellbeing. Not one of them comes to the Earth without their network in place around them. It may be that those circumstances you describe are necessary to help them to face and walk through their fear. They are just the challenges that are needed to bring them into the true expression of their beings.

Lynn: I think the thing is I was just concerned that you could have children who were frightened or worried. But I guess it not my job to walk another's path?

And what is harder is that sometimes they are forced into a pretence because those around them do not understand. But even that is part of their challenge.

Never think that anyone ever walks alone. Certainly not one who has undertaken life for a purpose of love and service.

It is the same answer I give to so many questions, I am afraid. It is something which needs thought from the spirit mind not from a physical understanding alone.

Fear of Psychic Ability

Stella: From the time I first had memory to possibly up until my twenties I was always what they called psychic. I always had the knowledge of the other people around me and I was quite happy with it. It was a normal way of life to me then. Then all of a sudden for no reason that I understand, I got frightened and I went for about 20-25 years before I actually came back to start learning more about what psychic actually meant to me. I didn't recapture the early parts because I had outgrown that but I started walking the path again. Now is that a sort of opting out and coming back within one life?

No. That is a learning, because the second part was walking through choice, wasn't it? You had made the choice. It was in the release, in the letting go, that you discovered the true nature and the belonging.

It is necessary to understand fear and you cannot understand fear without experiencing it.

Lynn: I think, sometimes though, fear is not a conscious choice for people; they do not see it as that. It is within them but they haven't labelled it as that and I think that can be quite difficult.

But it is always a conscious choice or was at one time. Perhaps in the darkness they have even lost the knowledge of when the choice was made so it seems an unconscious thing.

Lynn: I was thinking of children.

It is even then a continuation of life. It is always an outworking but an outworking that you will never see fully viewed only from the physical life.

Always it is, at one point, a conscious choice but we can so lose ourselves within the maze of darkness that we really cannot even see the starting point. There are always those there to help us back to it and there is no time limit on how long it takes because the time measurement is purely physical.

Experience, release and trust are the stepping stones to understanding.

Schizophrenia – is this a distorted psychic ability?

Lynn: It occurred to me that schizophrenia - where people hear voices - is that a spirit link which is a bit off beam or is that something to do with the physical body?

Nearly always those who are diagnosed with it have a sensitivity and sometimes, although not always, there is amassed a psychic power within them. If they are frightened of it and do not know how to release it, it can cause them to lose faith in their foundation and so open themselves to other influences.

There is another category where perhaps the links are misunderstood and, in the misunderstanding, they are opened in a wrong way. Although great help is always given it cannot be imposed and if it is rejected it can lead to such problems.

There are other influences which, at times, cause confusion. It is an inability to balance within the self all of the many strands which make an individual. Some cases - indeed many cases - have a foundation there, but there are many other categories.

Another main category is where some reject the light and open their beings to darkness, but even that is a journey of experience. The experience of it will, when the time is right, bring them to a much greater understanding of themselves and their pathways. God allows each one the experiences that they need and we must do that too.

It is an area where there is a great deal more understanding needed. Many quite different things are put in a little box labelled 'schizophrenia'. They are quite different in origin, in need and, indeed, in overcoming.

Using Hypnotherapy to Overcome a Fear

Lynn: Some people have used hypnotherapy to try to remove a fear and it seems have been successful but have they really overcome it?

Sometimes an irrational fear, e.g. fear of the dark, fear of spiders etc., is held. This could be just the physical manifestation of something held within the spirit centre. It is possible by revealing the incident that gave rise to the physical fear, there is a means to deal it. Then, that manifestion of fear would be overcome but inner fear will come out in other ways because the root of the fear has not been faced.

Consider a rose. Perhaps that rose has some leaves on it that have the disease called black spot on them. You can pull off those leaves and it will be gone, won't it? But it will certainly come back because the root cause has not been dealt with. With the rose perhaps it comes back as black spot again but in your own beings the fear could well be manifest as something completely different. It does not have to be the same manifestation of the fear, but it is the same root. It is the difference between dealing with the manifestation and dealing with the cause.

However, sometimes seeking the help and taking the help is an important step on the pathway and the small overcoming could be a major step forward. It is neither 'right' nor 'wrong', but, like many other things, an option to be considered.

Meridian Lines

Stella: We read of meridian lines in various different concepts. Are these purely physical or are they part of our spirit that we can use for healing within either the physical or spiritual aspect?

What is within any part of your being is within all of your being in one form or another. In all life there are little balances, balance within balance, until we are in the universal balance - God.

What you are expressing as meridian lines with the physical effects upon your physical bodies, have an equivalent energy field in each other part of your beings, and in every other field of existence. Balance within balance, and what you do to any one part affects the whole.

So the answer to your question is yes. As to how you can affect it, think of the pebble in the pond. Put the pebble into the part you can reach and the ripples go through the whole.

Stella: So if we give healing that we think is for a pain in the body, we may actually be touching something held deeper in the mind, like fear?

And in all of the other little layers, too, pain in the body, fear from the mind, anger from the emotions, and any other dis-ease. No one part stands alone, each one is an element of a whole.

How could you come into total knowledge and understanding and expression of that whole unless you learned to come into that understanding within individual parts? That is the purpose of these little facets of life, like your physical lives, giving you the opportunity to come into just one understanding. Great experience is needed to find the greater reality.

Advice for the worried or depressed

Stella: We see people around us who are walking very difficult pathways and are worn down by depression and worry, especially for family members who seem to have lost their way. Have you any advice for them?

The best advice is to let go the fear. I know it is hard to do but all things have their purpose and outcomes are not always what they seem. There are always many helping. To anyone I would say open your being and when you clear the fear you, too, will find that you are able to direct that light to those whom you love and those whom you care for and, indeed, to change the world around you.

I know it is difficult to maintain the peace within you but the Master said 'my peace I give to you, my peace I leave with you.' Remember, too, that the peace of God is beyond all understanding and indeed is with us always. It is only ourselves who can take us out of the perception of this peace.

You might find it useful to develop a little something, a little prayer, a little mantra, a few words, anything that will have the meaning for you of 'peace'. When you say them, feel the peace coming over you and flowing through you. You will find each time you do this, the feeling becomes stronger and stronger until the time comes when you do not need the little mantra any more.

Do not judge yourself harshly. By doing so you are restricting help that the loving beings who walk with you can give.

Fading of Life on Planets

Stella: We are told that it is possible that some planets even in our Solar System might once have sustained life. Could that have happened?

Life itself, true life is eternal but the different facets of life are not. They have beginnings and endings and the places where that life is experienced also have beginnings and endings. But often the life, for example physical life upon the Earth, has a much shorter time span than the planet itself and that is for a reason.

For a start, there is a natural evolution that seems a very long period from your Earth time perspective but seems simply like a new baby being born from the spiritual one. There have been and there are many similar places of living and experiencing, even now within God's realm. There have been many in the past and there will be many others in the future.

Some no longer support life forms, because life forms have free will and there are points along the way where decisions must be made. The cumulative effect of these decisions is to create a force and once this force has gained a certain momentum, there is no turning back. Therefore, if the understanding of the damage that the particular race is causing has not been reached before that momentum has gathered, then there is only one way and that is extinction of the indigenous life in that place. But the true life goes on and whilst the learning is needed, other places will be created and will be ready for the learning to go on.

The benefit of these places of learning, like the beautiful Earth, is that within the total freedom and the greater perception that you associate with life in spirit, there is not the opportunity to discover for yourself, from a confined state, something that is apparent from spirit perspective. So a physical life allows an individual to meet a challenge, overcome it and to reach a new point of understanding.

Therefore, it is necessary to have these places of experience. Yes, the Earth is one but there are others. While they are needed they will be provided until the time comes when the beings upon the places of experience will realise that they hold the keys to the memory, to allowing and perpetuating their place for others to use.

Prayer for the Dark Places

Thank God for the heights that we have soared, for the love generated, filling and transforming each being enjoined and raising them into the knowledge of the beauty of the universe.

Ask that this light and joy may be carried to the dark places of the world to those who hold themselves in darkness, frightened of the light. Send that gentle light and love, in trust, to be used by those whose mission it is to reach out, without judgement, to help those so in need.

It is by giving that we receive. It is by healing that we are healed.

Facing Life's Challenges

Think of many of your little mountains, little in God's scale of things even the largest of them. When climbed, there are many points that are facing towards the top and appear to be peaks. When that peak has been reached then it is seen that there is a little bit more to go before the real top is reached.

On your journeys through life you achieve many such peaks. Then you have a resting time before you set off to scale the next height. When one peak has been conquered – one challenge overcome – you earn the right to see the next one open before you. But there is always the resting time and there is always the time to enjoy and reflect, the reward time.

Chapter 9

The Way Ahead

"The more you go in trust, the less you will be frightened to trust. You will know that part of God's trust to you is that you are protected along the pathway."

Introduction

We are aware that we walk different pathways during our lives, both physically and spiritually. It isn't always easy to recognise the point of change or to know if the way we have chosen is 'right' for us. Brother always tells us that the choice is simple – but never easy! Here, he speaks to us about the way ahead.

New Pathways

Lynn: How can we know when we have started on a new pathway?

Do not look for that blinding light as on the road to Damascus which changes everything. Although it may well be like that within your spirit self, within your physical consciousness it is one step at a time.

You walk through new doorways. You walk along the new way before you are aware of what it is and you are some way into the new pathway before it really takes shape and you even perceive that you are, indeed, on a new way. You must find the detail in your own time. It will unfold as you walk in trust.

The more you go in trust, the less you will be frightened to trust. You will know that part of God's trust to you is that you are protected along the pathway. That will not keep you from your necessary experiences and opportunities and testing times, but it will protect you within the pathway of service, uphold you and keep you safe in loving hands.

A Step in Trust

Stella: Sometimes there are periods when everything seems very difficult and we can't seem to break out of the negativity. I suppose this is for a purpose?

Sometimes your pathways appear beset with difficulties. Sometimes it seems that just as one thing is overcome, you turn around and there are several other things besetting you. When that happens, rejoice, for you earned the right to overcome. I know it is not easy to see that with physical eyes alone, but every single challenge that you meet you are capable of overcoming. More than that, you have earned the right because it is only through the overcoming that understanding is achieved and progress is made.

I do not expect you to say 'Oh good another problem!'

When you are able to view without mists, to see fully with your spirit eyes and look at your physical pathway of challenges, you will say 'I did not think I was ready for that, I did not think I had done what was necessary to reach that part but I see now and I rejoice'. When you accept that you take a step in trust.

Do not allow the tempter within to unsettle your base. Do not allow the part of you within yourselves, which is that tempter, to disturb the trust. Know that you walk that pathway of challenge because you are ready for the opportunities that it brings. When you are in need of a little respite that beautiful spirit mist will close down around you and create you the space, love, wellbeing and the golden light to re-energise you and allow you to take the next step with renewed vigour and trust in the outcome.

Let go of worry. There are many with you, holding your hands and ensuring that you cannot fall. Go in trust.

Advent – Preparation & Waiting

Stella asked Brother if he would explain a little more about Advent, which he has told us is a very special and important time. This is his reply.

We speak of the advent, the coming and the preparation for the coming. Who does this preparation? Who is waiting for the coming? It is each of us. It is a very personal thing and it is a universal thing. It is a re-enactment of the first coming but it is fresh and new each time. It is the time of opening. Oh yes, you have received the Christ light before; yes, the Christ light is within you. Why then, you may say, do you have to be open to receive it again?

Stella: We need a top up.

We each receive according to our capacity. From that receiving, we walk on our pathways - hopefully expanding and growing - until we reach a point where it is time, once more, to prepare to open, to receive according to our greater capacity. That is why 're-enactment' is really the wrong word as each time of coming is new and unique. We are not just *renewing* the light we have already received, we are receiving according to a greater capacity. If you are prepared and have made your temple of light ready, then it will be easier to take in that new light and to allow it to shine.

If the preparation has not been done and there are places of darkness within you, things unresolved, things that are against truth, then the capacity for the light will be diminished, therefore the receiving will be diminished.

Do you see how important the preparation is? Do you see how important Advent is?

Do you see that, in the preparation, in the waiting, you are uniting with so many loving beings who are taking similar steps, who have taken them and who will take them?

What is the preparation? It is the inner cleansing, the clearing out, opening to the light of truth. You see, truth is light.

When truth is not embraced then mists and darkness are being held. Therefore the light that comes has to work at dispelling them rather than working for the advancement of your personal way, for the good of the universe and for illuminating the pathway leading you closer to the knowledge of God.

Truth is a great step in the cleansing and to embrace truth, not just on an individual scale but on a universal one, means that the light shines freely without obstacles throughout the universe. That is part of the preparation to receive.

Where does the receiving take place? Inside the temple of our spiritual hearts, our spirit selves.

How do we reach it? By going into the silence and by existing even for a moment in the infinity of the universal love which is at the heart of that temple.

Embrace the waiting. Embrace the preparation time. Know that it is a vital and essential part of the coming of the Christ light to be received according to your capacity, received as it was in the beginning, as it will ever be.

Embrace the preparation and open to receive that light, for when in your contemplations you can enter into your inner temples you will experience an infinity of love.

It is a very precious flower. Do not overlook it. Use it. Be ready, and, in that preparation carry the excitement that the shepherds did; open to the golden light of the angels who gather round you. It is indeed a precious time that will lead you to the birth of the new Christ light within your manger, your stable, your place within God's universe.

There are those who prepare and prepare and prepare but are not prepared to see. They are not willing to see and receive what comes because they carry an image of something different. They miss the joy of the receiving because it is not what they expected to receive and they do not recognise it.

If you look back to the birth of Jesus, many were waiting for the coming of a king. They did not recognise the Christ light in the little being because it wasn't what was expected.

Be careful always that the preparation, as important as it is, doesn't become more important than the receiving. That is another lesson and it is one that all need to watch out for.

Embrace your advent. Be aware of what it is you are preparing for and what you are celebrating. Do so with joy and love and anticipation as it was at the first coming.

A New Pathway

Stella: Sometimes we feel we have found a new pathway. Is there any such thing?

At various stages on your journey through life you find a new way. I say a 'new' way, but it is really another part of the path you are walking, newly revealed to you. When it happens you start experiencing the opening of your spirit consciousness even further, even while you are within the confines of the physical state and, when there has been sufficient experiencing, there will be another point of understanding reached. Another height scaled.

You speak of scaling heights as an achievement. But sometimes it is in the coming down the other side that you get your rewards, isn't it? When you are climbing up a mountain, what do you see? You see the mountain face large before you.

You do not even really have the ability to look around as you need to be concentrating on the climb. Even if you did, all you would see is the sky and the mountain face.

It is after you have reached the summit and you start to descend that you see before you a landscape opening that perhaps you have never seen or experienced before. For each height you scale you earn the right to walk down the other side. You may decide before you have gone very far that you wish to go up another height and that is the way of growth. There is no pathway that is simply up and up.

You often speak of the cycles of life. But you tend to equate the up with reaching up to what you call the heavens and the down with some form of descent into a physical confinement. But even that is an illusion of your conscious mind. You need to experience the whole of God's world, of God's universe.

You achieve what is necessary from the physical aspect. You walk through many facets of experience of which your physical existence is but one small part. You will learn to see it as just one aspect of learning.

Then you will understand the illusion of their being many new pathways. But, illusion or not, each experience is fresh and new because always you are at a unique place in your own unique journey through life and on your own path to God.

The Journey Has Begun

The journey has begun. The route has been selected.
The journey to where?

The journey has begun. You have covered the first part.
When did it start?

The journey has begun. Of that there is no doubt.
What is this journey?
It started with consciousness. It travels through awareness.
It leads to fulfilment. It leads to God.

But God is with you always. God is on the journey.
God is in your first consciousness. So what is this journey?

What can it be, this journey that you are on?
You do not know where you have been.
You do not know where you will go.
But you know that you are going and that is enough.

For at every stage something is unfolding. The knowledge within
you is growing. What is that knowledge?
The knowledge of God.

Call it then the journey to a beauteous spirit, to
a great unfolding, to a freedom, to a wide horizon, to light, to
beauty, to love and peace expressed -

- To the knowledge of your God.

Closing Prayer

Oh Great Spirit, creator God, we thank you for the steps we have taken. We thank you for the pieces of the puzzle found and the joy of the knowledge that we have within us, each one, the means to put them together and create a bright and loving whole.

We thank you for the enjoining of loving beings upon the physical plane wherever they may be and upon the spirit plane, perceived or not.

We thank you for the little understandings because little understandings together enable us to conquer mighty things. We thank you for those little things because we know they are first steps towards understanding.

We thank you for the mighty framework of pure love which upholds, guides, supports and leads us to God.

We ask your blessing and protection around each one. That each one may be empowered to do their work, whatever that work may be.

We ask in the name of the Master, Our Lord Jesus the Christ. We pray Thy will be done.

Amen.

God Bless you and peace be with you.

APPENDIX

Brother frequently speaks of the importance of meditation and the opportunities for advancement on every level that it offers us. Listed below are some of his words given as thoughts for meditation.

Thoughts for Meditation

- Change is a measure of progress. There is no advancement without change.

- Change is a simple fact of existence. Denying change is denying reality.

- Magnetism is a physical law of attraction. Similarly, there is a spiritual law of attraction which means that every being attracts whatever and whoever they need in order to experience what is necessary for the next stage of the journey.

- Understanding only comes after discovery and experience. It is a natural law of life.

- Make your daily prayer, "Please forgive me. I forgive."

- The only true barriers in life are the boundaries of your own consciousness.

- Remember all the hurts of the past are gone. Only their lessons remain.

- Part of each human pathway is to overcome.

- Without each other we could not fulfil our potential.

- How can we truly test ourselves without things to overcome?

- There is nothing within God's realm that is not operating according to the universal law of giving and receiving.

- Pain is a part of learning.

- Heaven is now. Do not miss it by constantly looking ahead.

Rose Meditation

You may find it useful to record Brother's words so that you can play them back while concentrating fully on the meditation.

Never do meditation while driving or operating machinery of any kind.

Turn off the telephone before you start and try to ensure that you have a time where you will not be interrupted.

Most of all, enjoy the experience!

This guided meditation is a transcript of Brother's words.

Sit or lay down with your back and your head comfortably supported. Close your eyes.

First you must ensure that the physical body is perfectly balanced so stretch out every limb as hard as you can, tense every muscle and let go. Relax - if you feel any irritation anywhere then stretch that muscle again, tense and let go. When you are sure that you have dealt with any physical irritations turn your attention to your breathing.

Breathe in as deeply as you can, hold the breath and breathe out, do this several times.

As you breathe in feel the cool, cool flow of the precious life-giving air entering your body, entering your lungs, doing work that only it can.

Feel the new life from the oxygen flowing through your veins touching every part of your body with every inward breath. Each time, breathe in more deeply and fully. Each breath takes you closer to that centre part of your existence where you are at one with all of life.

Now you are in that part, continue breathing steadily, naturally.

122

As you breathe in a vision fills your eyes, a vision of a perfectly formed bed of roses. Everywhere you look you see these perfect roses, perfect flowers, perfect stems, perfect leaves, perfect forms, abundant flowers. Everywhere you look their colour fills your vision, their fragrance fills your senses.

In your mind's eye, select one and go into it. You are at one with it. Feel its life flow through you.

First, look at the root which plants it firmly in the earth. The root spreads out in all directions and takes precious water as a gift from the earth. It takes the nourishment and goodness which is freely offered to it from the ground in which it grows.

Each part of that root finds its own place where it is welcomed and it takes the gifts which are given to it and it gives them to the stem so that the stem grows stronger. It grows upwards to the light. You are part of that stem, you are one with it. You feel the growth through all of your veins, through all of your body. You feel yourself getting taller and stronger. You feel that you are this channel of support which has found its purpose in life to sustain beauty, for if there were no stem there could be no leaves or flowers stretching joyously upwards and outwards to the light.

Feel this reaching upwards and outwards to the beckoning light. As that happens, be aware of little branches growing out from the stem, and, from them, oh what wonders of perfectly formed green, green leaves, each one unique, each one a myriad pattern of life-supporting veins. Just as you have arms so the stem has leaf branches and leaves and they too reach upwards and outwards adding to the wholeness of this special plant, giving beauty and receiving the wondrous rays of the sun and the cool, cool droplets of the dew. But still that central stem stretches higher and higher until a new life comes from it, the delicate life of the flower bud. It is full of beauty, full of colour, a life that is whole in itself but consists of many, many petals, each one a mass of life-supporting veins.

You are at one with the petals. You have a sense of wholeness and oneness with the flower. You are enclosed by petals.

The bright, bright yellow of the pollen sends its glow throughout your petals. See the glow as you look at your body, the glow of that bright pollen. It is as though, one at a time, the petals unfold to reveal what is hidden within, the centre of beauty and wholeness.

You are at one with the wholeness of the flower. You are at one with nature all around and, as you enjoy this feeling of wonder, so your vision once again builds with many, many, many roses - roses of every colour, of every form, each one perfect, each one glorifying in its beauty and perfection. You are at one in the harmony of the rose.

You are at one with each rose, with each petal which links each stem and each root. You rejoice in the oneness. You rejoice in the wholeness and you watch as this vision of roses merges into one pure white shining rose. And that is yours to keep with you, within your mind and within your heart.

When you are ready, be aware, once again, of the movement of your breath. With each inward breath, come more fully back into your physical mind consciousness until you are ready to open your eyes and bring your new found sense of peace and harmony into your everyday life.

Guidance CDs

These CDs are extracts from recorded sessions of conversations following regular weekly meditations with Brother. His words are channelled through Phyllis McCarthy and the conversations are with Stella McCarthy, Lynn and Alastair Buchan. Although the group are Christian, the wisdom and advice is relevant to everyone, regardless of culture or religion. It truly transcends barriers and is concerned with an individual's relationship with self, with all life and with God.

We are sharing his channelled wisdom and love in the expectation that it will help others as it has helped us. Four CDs are currently available, Belonging, Prayer, Healing and Fear. Please note – they are recordings of actual sessions so are not of studio quality. The sound quality varies and the volume levels may need a little adjustment for different tracks.

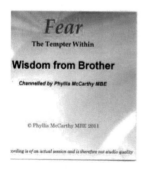

Fear Contents

Track 1 Opening Prayer (Brother)

Track 2 Fear – the Tempter Within (Brother)

Track 3 Fear Meditation by Stella McCarthy

Track 4 Closing Prayer (Brother)

Healing Contents
Track 1 Opening Prayer (Brother)
Track 2 Healing (Brother)
Track 3 Healing Meditation by
Stella McCarthy
Track 4 Closing Prayer

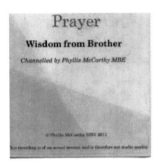

Prayer Contents
Track 1 Opening Prayer (Brother)
Track 2 The Effectiveness of
Prayer (Brother)
Track 3 The Lord's Prayer,
Brother's interpretation
Track 4 Guided Meditation by
Stella McCarthy
Track 5 Closing Prayer (Brother)

Belonging Contents
Track 1 Opening Prayer and
Theme (Brother)
Track 2 Answer to Question on
Learning (Brother)
Track 3 Guided Meditation by
Brother
Track 4 Closing Prayer (Brother)

NB This is an older recording made
on older recording equipment

Section Index

Editor's Note

We hope you found this book helpful in your personal quest for spiritual knowledge and development. You will find some more of the words and excerpts of recordings made at the meditation circles on the Brother's Way website: www.brothersway.co.uk. CDs of extracts from the sessions, including meditations, are available from the website, price £5, just to cover the production and postage costs. Further books on Brother's teachings are to follow soon. Meditation, Healing and Crystal Workshops based on Brother's Way are also held at various times – details can be found on the website.

Our hope is that, like us, you will find a new door open on the most important quest of your life – the path to self-knowledge and the path to God.

God bless your journey in whatever way you wish to take it.

Phyllis McCarthy
Stella McCarthy
Lynn Buchan

Email: booksatbway.gmail.com